The China-U.S. Trade War

Lawrence Lau's book on the current U.S.-China trade war and the possible trajectories for this critical relationship in the coming decades is superb. It is insightful, balanced and comprehensive; rich in data on trade, investment, science and technology, and it is essential reading for anyone who wants to get past the headlines to understand the relative strengths, vulnerabilities, and crucially the scope for a beneficial mix of strategic, economic and technological cooperation and competition, between these two great economies in the future. Professor Lau is unmatched in his depth of understanding of these two economic giants.

—**A. Michael Spence**
Nobel Laureate in Economic Sciences (2001)
Senior Fellow, The Hoover Institution, Stanford University

This beautifully composed book uses nontechnical language to unravel the intricacies of the 2018 U.S.-China trade war, together with its long-term impact. I learned a lot from reading it.

—**Chen-Ning Yang**
Nobel Laureate in Physics (1957)

U.S.-China trade relations are right now as important as any global economic issue and as any bilateral U.S.-China issue. Lawrence Lau brings light in the form of rigorous honest fact-based economic analysis to a subject where most of the discussion has been heated bluster, false claims, and political rhetoric. This is the right book to read for anyone who wants to understand the U.S.-Chinese relations or the global economy.

—**Lawrence H. Summers**
Former U.S. Secretary of the Treasury
Former President, Harvard University

This is a timely and penetrating analysis of the China-U.S. trade and economic relations, from its origins to its impacts and to a way forward. All who are concerned about today's most important bilateral relationship in the world will learn from Professor Lawrence Lau's insightful book.

—**Yingyi Qian**
Chairman of the Council, Westlake University
Former Dean, School of Economics and Management, Tsinghua University
Counsellor of the State Council, People's Republic of China

Everyone, everywhere, is potentially affected by events in the world's two largest economies, the United States and China. As relations between them fray, Lawrence J. Lau's timely *The China-U.S. Trade War and Future Economic Relations* is full of careful analysis, penetrating insight and helpful suggestions from the world's preeminent economist on this relationship.

—**Michael J. Boskin**
Tully M. Friedman Professor of Economics, Stanford University
Former Chair, U.S. President's Council of Economic Advisers

The trade war between the United States and China has been dominated by the sometimes heated rhetoric of both the press and some of the government officials responsible in the two countries for determining trade policies. This sober and systematic study of U.S.-China trade relations and of technological development in the two countries is particularly timely. Lawrence Lau is one of the world's foremost economists working on these issues. In this study, he provides an in-depth analysis of the likely economic impact of the trade war on the overall economic performance of the two countries (modest and readily manageable) and of the relative progress of technological innovation in the two countries. This study should be read carefully by anyone working on these issues for their governments, for the press, as well as any individual citizen who wants to understand the issues.

—**Dwight H. Perkins**
Harold Hitchings Burbank Professor of Political Economy, Emeritus
Former Chair, Department of Economics, Harvard University

The history of Sino-American relations, to a great extent, has been a shared history. A major motivation for American interest in China since their war for independence was their obsession with the "China market". Yet the so-called "China market" existed only as a myth since from the arrival of the "Empress of China" in 1784 till 1978, America's trade with China was only a tiny dot in American foreign trade. Now when U.S.-China trade reached such an important level for both countries, President Trump launched a trade war against China. Lawrence Lau's timely and penetrating study will tell us it is still in best interest for both countries if they continue to pursue a shared journey and destination instead of parting ways. Anyone who believes in a better shared future of the world should read this great book and read it carefully.

—**Xu Guoqi**
Kerry Group Professor in Globalization History, The University of Hong Kong
Author of *Chinese and Americans: A Shared History*

THE CHINA-U.S. TRADE WAR

AND FUTURE ECONOMIC RELATIONS

LAWRENCE J. LAU

THE CHINESE UNIVERSITY PRESS

The China-U.S. Trade War and Future Economic Relations
 By Lawrence J. Lau

First edition   2019
Second printing   2019

ISBN: 978-988-237-112-5

Published by:
The Chinese University Press
The Chinese University of Hong Kong
Sha Tin, N.T., Hong Kong.
Fax: +852 2603 7355
Email: cup@cuhk.edu.hk
Website: www.chineseupress.com

Printed in Hong Kong

To Ayesha, my muse, my love and my life

.

Contents

Part I

Understanding the Trade War: History, Facts and Potential Impacts

Foreword

Tung Chee-Hwa

Vice-Chairman,
Chinese People's Political Consultative Conference National Committee
Chairman, China-U.S. Exchange Foundation

The year 2018 marks the 40th anniversary of the beginning of the highly successful Chinese economic reform. However, it is also the start of the China-U.S. trade war. The United States and China are the largest and the second largest economies in the world respectively. They are also the largest and the second largest trading nations in the world. Between the two of them, they are the most important trading partners for most of the countries in the world. The China-U.S. economic relationship is the most important bilateral relationship in the world today. If China and the U.S. work together towards a common goal, almost anything is possible. If they work at cross-purposes, then little is possible.

Professor Lawrence Lau, the author of this book, is an old friend of mine. We have known each other since the 1980s. He was born on the Mainland, raised in Hong Kong, went to the U.S. for college and taught at Stanford University as a Professor of Economics for 40 years. In 2004, he returned to Hong Kong to serve as the Vice-Chancellor and President of The Chinese University of Hong Kong (CUHK). In 2010, he became the Chairman of CIC International (Hong Kong) Co., Ltd., a wholly-owned subsidiary of China Investment Corporation, the sovereign wealth fund of China. He also began to serve concurrently as the Ralph and Claire Landau Professor of Economics at CUHK, a position he continues to hold today on a part-time basis.

Professor Lau specialises in economic development, economic growth, and the economies of East Asia, including that of China. In 1966, he developed the first econometric model of China, and has continued to revise and update his model since.

In 1979, less than a year after the beginning of Chinese economic reform and opening, Professor Lau visited the Mainland for the first time since he was two years old, as a member of a delegation of the American Economic Association. His delegation shared their knowledge with the Chinese economic policy-makers at the time. Since then, Professor Lau has continued to offer advice to Chinese economic policy-makers at the most senior level.

Professor Lau is no stranger to China-U.S. economic relations. In the 1990s, he, together with Professor K. C. Fung, were the first economists to try to reconcile the differences between the official Chinese and U.S. estimates of the China-U.S. trade balance. Their research results were used by former Chinese Premier Zhu Rongji. In the 2000s, he introduced the idea of measuring the China-U.S. trade balance in terms of the domestic value-added generated by exports rather than the gross value of exports that the two countries send each other. The research was carried out together with a team at the Chinese Academy of Sciences led by Professor Chen Xikang, with the finding that the resulting U.S.-China trade deficit is reduced by approximately one half. Professor Lau also contributed to the study, *U.S.-China 2022: U.S.-China Economic Relations in the Next Ten Years—Towards Deeper Engagement and Mutual Benefit*, commissioned by the China-U.S. Exchange Foundation.

There is no topic that is more important, more timely or more urgent than the China-U.S. trade war. Professor Lau is the ideal person to write about the implications of the China-U.S. trade war and the proposed resolution. He is rigorous on facts and figures. He knows both economies well. He understands both the Chinese and the U.S. points of view. And he has a balanced perspective. He remains optimistic, as I am, that with coordination, collaboration and cooperation, the China-U.S. trade imbalance can be successfully reduced and even eliminated by increasing U.S. exports to China. China-U.S. economic relations can not only be win-win for both countries, but also bring great benefits for the rest of the world.

Preface

The relationship between China and the United States is arguably the most important as well as the most critical bilateral relationship in the world today. The U.S. is the largest economy and the mightiest military power in the world. China is the second largest economy, the most populous nation and a significant nuclear power. If China and the U.S. work together as partners towards a common goal, many things are possible. However, if they confront each other constantly, a war may eventually ensue, and the resulting devastations are unthinkable. There are no winners in a nuclear war. It is therefore important for bilateral relations to be carefully managed by both countries, so that any unnecessary confrontation can be avoided.

In writing this book, I have three basic objectives. First, I want to show that while the real effects of the China-U.S. trade war in 2018 are not negligible, they are relatively manageable for China and even more so for the U.S. This is true even if the new U.S. tariffs eventually cover all U.S. imports from China. There is no need to panic.

Second, I want to show that behind the trade war are potential economic and technological competition between China and the U.S. and the rise of populist, isolationist, nationalist and protectionist sentiments around the world, in particular in the U.S. The competition between China and the U.S. cannot be avoided and is likely to become the "new normal". However, my analysis shows that while in the aggregate the Chinese real GDP is likely to surpass the U.S. real GDP sometime in the 2030s, on a per capita basis China will still remain far, far behind and will not reach parity with the U.S. until the very end of the 21st century. Moreover, in terms of the overall level of scientific and technological development and innovative capacity in general, China still has a long road ahead to catch up to the U.S. As to the rise of xenophobia in both countries, it is up to each government to demonstrate not only by words but also by deeds that it is not necessary for anyone to lose from international trade and direct investment—that there is enough overall gain for everyone to benefit.

Third, I want to show that China-U.S. economic collaboration and cooperation is a potentially positive-sum game—both China and the U.S. can win at the same time. Given the economic complementarities between the two economies, both can benefit significantly through mutual trade and direct and portfolio investment, and especially through better-coordinated economic collaboration and cooperation, taking advantage of and fully utilising each other's currently idle or underutilised resources. Balancing China-U.S. trade is actually possible. Enhancing mutual economic inter-dependence will help to build trust and reduce the potential for conflict in the future.

In 1997, at the height of the East Asian currency crisis, I wrote an essay titled "The Sky Isn't Falling!", explaining why the Chinese economy should be able to manage, and in particular, why the Renminbi should not be devalued at that time. Indeed, the sky did not fall, the Renminbi did not devalue, and the Chinese economy wound up with a real rate of growth of approximately 8 percent. Since then, I have written under the same title a couple of times, immediately after the collapse of Lehman Brothers in the U.S. in September 2008, and also after the bursting of the Chinese stock market bubble and the unexpected devaluation of the Renminbi in 2015. The Chinese economy is large and resilient. The Chinese government is agile, flexible and pragmatic. It has many instruments at its disposal. It will be able to manage the fallouts from the trade war. There is no need to panic. The sky is not falling!

December 2018

Acknowledgments

I wish to thank my wife, Ayesha Macpherson Lau, for her constant encouragement as well as her insightful comments on many successive drafts of this book. I am also most grateful to Mr. Tung Chee-Hwa for his staunch support of this research, and particularly for taking the time from his extremely busy schedule to write a foreword for this book. I am indebted to Prof. Michael Boskin, Prof. Xikang Chen, Prof. Leonard Cheng, Dr. Stan Cheung, Prof. Terence Chong, Prof. Kwok-Chiu Fung, Prof. Ambrose Y. C. King, Prof. Pak-Wai Liu, Ms. Xiaomeng Peng, Prof. Dwight Perkins, Prof. Yingyi Qian, Prof. Condoleezza Rice, Prof. Michael Spence, Prof. Joseph Stiglitz, Prof. Lawrence Summers, Mr. Junjie Tang, Prof. Yanyan Xiong, Mr. Ting-Hin Yan, Prof. Chen-Ning Yang and Prof. Huanhuan Zheng for their invaluable advice, assistance, contributions and support, without which this book would not have been possible. I am also most grateful to my colleagues at The Chinese University Press, who worked tirelessly to put this book out in record time—Ms. Qi Gan, Dr. Ying Lin, Ms. Sushan Chan, Ms. Tian Chen, Mr. Justin Wai-Hin Cheung, Ms. Tsz-Yan Cho, Ms. Xiao Lin, Mr. Daniel Ng, Ms. Winifred Sin, Ms. Ting-Ting Tsoi, Ms. Angelina Wong, Ms. Minlei Melinda Ye and Mr. Brian Yu. Their dedication and efficiency set the highest professional standards. Of course, I retain sole responsibility for any remaining errors and for all opinions expressed herein, which do not necessarily reflect the views of any of the organisations with which I am or have been affiliated.

List of Illustrations

Tables

1. Introduction

The relation between China and the United States is arguably the most important bilateral relation in the world today. The U.S. and China are respectively the largest and the second largest economies in the world.[1] They are also respectively the largest and the second largest trading nations in the world, as well as each other's most important trading partner. If China and the U.S. work together as partners towards a common goal, many things are possible. An example is the Paris Agreement on the prevention of climate change, approved unanimously by 196 states and other parties in December 2015. This was possible only because both former U.S. President Barack Obama and Chinese President Xi Jinping worked together to make it happen. There are other similarly important global objectives that can be accomplished by the two countries working together as partners, such as the alleviation of poverty in Africa, the denuclearisation of the Korean Peninsula, the enhancement of global cyber-security, and further liberalisation of international trade and investment around the world.

Notwithstanding the tremendous economic progress that China has made since its economic reform and opening in 1978, its GDP per capita in

---

1   In any reference to economic data, China should be understood to mean the mainland of China only (not including Hong Kong, Macau and Taiwan). According to some "purchasing-power-parity" (PPP) estimates produced by the International Monetary Fund and the World Bank, China is already the world's largest economy, with the U.S. in second place. However, there are methodological problems with using such PPP estimates of GDP as a basis for the comparison of the real magnitudes of economic output across countries. See the discussion in Lawrence J. Lau (2007).

2017 was only US$9,137, still under the middle-income country threshold of US$12,000, and ranking below the 70th position in the world, compared to a GDP of US$59,518 per capita in the U.S.[2] China's overall military strength and scientific and technological capabilities still lag significantly behind the U.S. The Renminbi, the Chinese currency, cannot compare with the U.S. Dollar as an international medium of exchange or store of value. And even though China has veto power in the United Nations Security Council just like the U.S., its influence in multilateral organisations, such as the International Monetary Fund (IMF), the World Bank and the Asian Development Bank, is still relatively weak compared to not only that of the U.S. but also that of European countries and Japan. It is definitely too soon to speak of China and the U.S. as being a "Group of Two" or "G-2".

Moreover, despite China and the U.S. being each other's largest trading partner, there is still significant friction and potential conflict in their economic relations. The friction originated from U.S. grievances about the lopsided trade balance in China's favour, the allegedly undervalued exchange rate of the Renminbi, the lack of market access in China for U.S. firms, the perceived uneven playing field in Chinese markets that appears to favour Chinese state-owned enterprises (SOEs), the industrial policy of the China's government (as manifested in the "Made in China 2025" initiative), inadequate intellectual property-rights protection, forced technology transfer, cyber-theft of commercial and industrial information, and concerns about national security. These grievances culminated in the 2018 decision by U.S. President Donald Trump to impose three separate rounds of new U.S. tariffs on imports from China cumulatively worth US$250 billion, thus starting a trade war between the two countries.[3]

On 1 March 2018, President Trump announced a planned imposition

---

2   This is calculated by dividing the official U.S. GDP in 2017 by the official U.S. mid-year population in 2017.
3   This number has been changing. It started out being US$50 billion. As of 24 September 2018, it became US$250 billion. However, an additional US$267 billion has also been mentioned recently, bringing the potential total to US$517 billion, almost the same as the entire value of annual Chinese exports to the U.S.

of a 25 percent ad valorum[4] tariff on steel imports and a 10 percent ad valorum tariff on aluminium imports. China, which is not a significant direct exporter of steel or aluminium products to the U.S., nevertheless initiated a World Trade Organisation (WTO) complaint against these tariffs.[5] The first round of U.S. tariffs that specifically targeted China was on US$34 billion worth of Chinese imports, implemented on 6 July 2018, at a rate of 25 percent ad valorum, affecting goods such as airplane tires, water boilers, X-ray machine components and various other industrial parts. These tariffs were immediately met by retaliatory Chinese tariffs of 25 percent on US$34 billion worth of imports from the U.S., including goods such as electric vehicles, pork and soybeans. A second round of tariffs on another US$16 billion worth of imports from each other were implemented by both countries on 23 August 2018, again, at an ad valorum rate of 25 percent. China again filed a new complaint with the WTO about these new U.S. tariffs.

A third round of tariffs on US$200 billion worth of U.S. imports from China was imposed by the U.S. on 24 September 2018, at an initial rate of 10 percent, but to be raised to 25 percent on 1 January 2019. This latest round of tariffs brought the total value of U.S. imports from China subject to new U.S. tariffs equal to US$250 billion (34 + 16 + 200), or approximately half of the value of the total annual U.S. imports from China. China retaliated by imposing new tariffs on an additional US$60 billion worth of Chinese imports from the U.S., at various rates ranging from 5 to 25 percent, bringing the total value of Chinese imports from the U.S. subject to new Chinese tariffs to US$110 billion (34 + 16 + 60). Approximately US$40 billion worth of the remaining Chinese imports from the U.S., including large aircraft, integrated circuitry and semiconductors, are at the present time not subject to any new Chinese tariffs.

In addition, President Trump has threatened to impose additional tariffs on another US$267 billion worth of U.S. imports from China if China retaliates against the current U.S. tariffs. If implemented, this would mean

---

4   "Ad valorum" means according to the value.
5   The European Union filed a similar case with the WTO in June 2018.

the imposition of tariffs on a total of US$517 billion (250 + 267) worth of U.S. imports from China. U.S. imports of goods from China amounted to only US$505.6 billion in 2017, according to U.S. official statistics, and so this possible additional round of new tariffs, if implemented, will mean that the new U.S. tariffs will apply to all U.S. imports from China. However, it is still possible that some U.S. imports from China may be exempted from the new U.S. tariffs in order to protect U.S. firms and/or U.S. consumers. For example, approximately 10 percent of U.S. imports from China by value consists of Apple iPhones, which are assembled in China, and count as Chinese exports, even though the Chinese domestic value-added[6] content of Apple iPhones is very low, at less than 5 percent. Cell phones made in China have so far been exempted from the first three rounds of tariffs. Likewise, semiconductors imported from China to the U.S. are almost all products at the final-stage of finishing and packaging of semiconductors originally manufactured by U.S. high-tech firms for the U.S. market. Their Chinese domestic value-added contents are also very low. The costs of any new tariffs on these goods will therefore be borne primarily by U.S. firms such as Apple Inc. and consumers such as iPhone users, not by the Chinese contract manufacturers. Hence there is some uncertainty whether the new tariffs will be fully implemented.[7] It was reported that Presidents Trump and Xi reached a tentative truce agreement at their dinner meeting on the side-lines of the G-20 Summit in Buenos Aires, Argentina on 1 December 2018, suspending new or increased tariffs on both sides for 90 days to provide time for further negotiations.[8] This should be regarded as a hopeful development.

This China-U.S. trade war disrupts international trade and investment because of its effects not only on the Chinese and U.S. economies but also

---

6   The value-added amount of a firm is defined as the difference between its revenue and the cost of all its purchased inputs except labour. Thus, value-added consists of the sum of profits, wages and salaries, and depreciation. An assembly operation will typically have a low value-added to revenue ratio because a large quantity of intermediate inputs will have to be purchased elsewhere, most often from abroad.

7   Exemptions from the new tariffs may also be granted by the Office of the U.S. Trade Representative upon application by the importing firm.

8   Apparently, Presidents Trump and Xi also had telephone conversations with each other earlier in November to discuss issues of common concern prior to the G-20 Summit.

on the global supply chains that have sprung up and developed over the past decades. It causes great uncertainties for firms and households throughout the world in their consumption and investment decisions. It also has the potential of permanently altering China-U.S. relations.

* * * * *

This book has been written with three principal objectives in mind. First, we want to show that while the real effects of the China-U.S. trade war in 2018 are not negligible, they are relatively manageable for China and even more so for the U.S. This is true even if the new U.S. tariffs eventually cover all U.S. imports from China. There is no need to panic. However, the trade war will have psychological effects on the Chinese stock markets and on the exchange rate of the Renminbi, and it will negatively affect the confidence and expectations of Chinese enterprises and households.

Second, we want to show that behind the trade war is the potential economic and technological competition between China and the U.S., as well as the rise of populist, isolationist, and protectionist sentiments around the world, especially in the U.S. The competition between China and the U.S. in terms of being the largest economy in the world, as well as competition in the core technologies of the 21st century, such as artificial intelligence and quantum computing, probably cannot be avoided. It is likely to become the "new normal". However, our analysis shows that while in the aggregate China's real GDP is likely to surpass the U.S. real GDP sometime in the 2030s, on a per capita basis China will remain far, far behind the U.S. and will not reach parity with the U.S. until the end of the 21st century, if at all. Moreover, in terms of the overall general level of scientific and technological development and innovative capacity, China still has a long road ahead to catch up with the U.S. As to the rise of xenophobia in both countries, it is up to each government to demonstrate not only by words but also by actions that it is not necessary for anyone to lose from international trade and direct investments and that there is enough overall gain so that each will benefit. However, while international trade always benefits both trading-partner countries in the aggregate, it does create winners and losers within each country. Unfortunately, the market cannot redistribute part of the gains from the winners to the losers, and therefore government tax and expenditure policies for appropriate "redistribution" from the winners to the losers are necessary.

Third, we want to show that China-U.S. economic collaboration and cooperation is a potentially positive-sum game—both China and the U.S. can come out winners at the same time. Given the economic complementarities between the two economies, both can benefit significantly through mutual trade and direct and portfolio investments, and especially through better-coordinated economic collaboration and cooperation, taking advantage of and fully utilising each other's currently idle or underutilised resources. Balancing China-U.S. trade is actually possible. By increasing trade and investment between each other and hence enhancing mutual economic interdependence, it will help to build trust, reduce the potential for future conflict, and avoid the so-called "Thucydides Trap" of Professor Graham Allison, who argues that a China-U.S. war will be inevitable as a rising power challenges the dominance of an established power.[9]

The rise of the Chinese economy is a recent phenomenon. It began in late 1978, when China decided to undertake economic reform and opened its economy to international trade and investment. In retrospect, this was a momentous, correct and immensely successful decision on the part of China and its senior leaders, led by Deng Xiaoping, at the time. Chart 1.1 shows the shares of the U.S., the European Union, China, Japan, East Asia (excluding China and Japan) and India in world GDP from 1960 to 2017. The late Professor Angus Maddison estimates that China accounted for 30 percent of world GDP in the late 18th and early 19th centuries.[10] However, in 1960, China accounted for only 4.4 percent of world GDP. On the eve of its adoption of the policies of economic reform and opening to the world in 1978, China accounted for only 1.75 percent of world GDP, despite having one quarter of the world's population. China's share of world GDP declined

---

9   For a discussion of the "Thucydides Trap" as it applies to China-U.S. relations, see Graham T. Allison (2015).
10   See Angus Maddison (2006).

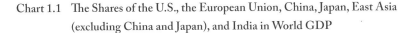

Chart 1.1   The Shares of the U.S., the European Union, China, Japan, East Asia
(excluding China and Japan), and India in World GDP

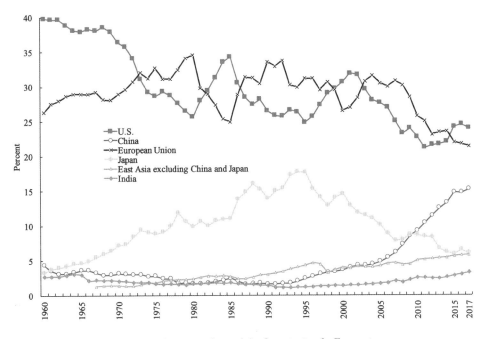

Sources: The World Bank national accounts data and the Organisation for Economic
Cooperation and Development (OECD) national accounts data files.

further to a nadir of less than 1.6 percent in 1987, but it then gradually
began to rise again, accelerating after its accession to the WTO in 2001. It
reached its current level of 15.2 percent in 2017.

By comparison, the U.S., which throughout this period was and still is
the largest economy in the world, accounted for 39.8 percent of world GDP
in 1960, but it saw its share decline to 24 percent by 2017. This was, however, not the result of a decline in the U.S. economy; rather, it was the result
of more rapid growth in other economies, especially those in East Asia[11],

---

11   East Asia, as used here, includes the countries of the Association of Southeast Asian
Nations (ASEAN) (Brunei, Cambodia, Indonesia, the Lao People's Democratic Re-
public, Malaysia, Myanmar, the Philippines, Singapore, Thailand and Vietnam), plus
Three (China including Hong Kong, Macau and Taiwan; the Republic of Korea; and
Japan).

including China. The share of world GDP in Japan, at one time the second largest and currently the third largest economy in the world, grew from 3.2 percent in 1960 to a peak of 17.7 percent in 1994, larger than China's share in 2017, but its share has since fallen to 6 percent. India's share, currently the fastest-growing major economy in the world, in terms of world GDP was 2.7 percent in 1960 and 3.2 percent in 2017, but it is expected to rise rapidly in the next decade or two.

Underlying these developments has been a gradual shift of the centre of gravity in the world economy from North America and Western Europe to East Asia, and within East Asia from Japan to China. The share of the U.S. and the nations comprising today's European Union combined, declined from almost two-thirds of world GDP in 1960 to 45 percent in 2017. In contrast, East Asia as a whole, which accounted for less than 10 percent of world GDP in 1960, today accounts for almost 30 percent. The U.S., the European Union, and East Asia are the three major economic blocs in the world today, each of which is approximately the same size, and together account for 75 percent of world GDP.

In international trade in goods and services, there has been a similar rise in East Asia's share. Chart 1.2 shows the shares of the U.S., the European Union, China, Japan, East Asia (excluding China and Japan) and India in world trade from 1960 to 2017. In 1960, the U.S. accounted for 15.8 percent of world trade, as befitting a large, continental economy with abundant natural resources of its own. By 2017, the U.S. share of world trade had declined to 11.5 percent. In contrast, China accounted for only 1.7 percent of world trade in 1960, and on the eve of its economic reform in 1978, China accounted for only 0.5 percent of world trade. The Chinese share of world trade rose gradually to 3 percent in 2000, just before its accession to the WTO, after which it grew to 10.2 percent in 2017. As a large continental economy like that of the U.S., the share of China in world trade is not likely to grow too much more in the future. The share of Japan in world trade declined from a peak of 7.6 percent in 1984 to 3.7 percent in 2016. The share of India grew from 1.3 percent in 1960 to 2.3 percent in 2017 and is expected to begin to grow more rapidly. Even though India is also a large economy, its share in world trade still has substantial room to grow.

Chart 1.2 The Shares of the U.S., the European Union, China, Japan, East Asia (excluding China and Japan) and India in World Trade in Goods and Services

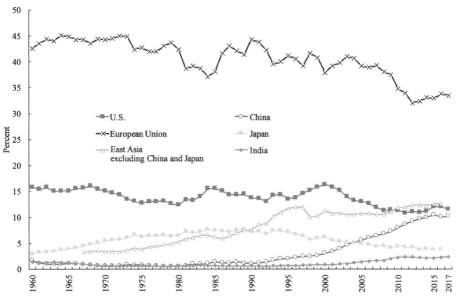

Sources: The World Bank national accounts data and OECD national accounts data files.

Worthy of note is the share of the European Union, which has remained high despite a drop from 42.5 percent in 1960 to 33.5 percent in 2017. However, this was in part the result of intra–European Union trade among its member-states that is still considered international trade, as opposed to the interstate trade in the U.S. and the inter-provincial trade in China, which are considered domestic trade. If the intra–European Union trade were netted out, the share of the European Union would look much more similar to that of China or the U.S. The combined share of the U.S. and the European Union in world trade was almost 60 percent in 1960 but it fell to 45.1 percent in 2017, almost the same as their combined share in world GDP; the East Asian share was 26.4 percent in 2016. The U.S., the European Union and East Asia together account for more than 70 percent of world trade. This once again shows that collectively the East Asian economies today have sufficient independent economic weight to balance the

U.S. and the European Union. Moreover, the East Asian economies have increasingly been exporting to and importing from one another, more than they have been exporting to or importing from the U.S. or Europe. This will help to reduce the economic dependence of the East Asian economies on the U.S. and Europe. Thus, they have become better able to weather and survive an economic downturn in the U.S. and Europe, as they did during the global financial crisis of 2008–2009 and the subsequent European sovereign debt crisis. This also supports the "partial-decoupling hypothesis", namely, that East Asia can continue to grow even while the U.S. and Europe are in an economic recession, and vice versa.

It is clear from this brief discussion that China has been a major beneficiary of its economic reform and opening to the world, which began in 1978. China's GDP and international trade in goods and services have both grown by leaps and bounds since. The rates of growth accelerated after China's exchange rate reform of 1994, which unified the multiple exchange rates, effectively devaluing the Renminbi, and made it current-account convertible. International trade and economic growth surged after China's accession to the WTO in 2001. However, the rate of growth of China's international trade has slowed noticeably during the past five years, as its wage rate and exchange rate rose and the rapidly rising demand from its own huge domestic market came into its own to become a major source of aggregate demand.

* * * * *

This book is organised as follows. In Chapter 2, we present a very brief review of some selected highlights of the history of the development of China-U.S. relations. In Chapter 3, adjusted—and in my opinion more reliable and comparable—estimates of the China-U.S. trade balance in goods and services, in both gross value and value-added terms, are presented. It is essential to know the true state of the China-U.S. trade balance before effective solutions can be devised to narrow the trade surplus or deficit. This chapter is a little technical and the reader may wish to skip it on a first reading, except to note that the adjusted estimates of the overall U.S.-China trade deficit for 2017 are US$254 billion in gross-value terms and US$111 billion in value-added terms, much lower than the often-quoted numbers.

The actual and potential impacts of the 2018 trade war between China and the U.S. on the two economies are analysed and discussed in Chapter 4. It is shown that the negative impacts are basically manageable for China, and even more so for the U.S. In Chapter 5, we show that the Chinese and U.S. economies are actually highly complementary, and therefore trade and investment between them should be highly beneficial to both. China and the U.S. make excellent economic partners for each other. In Chapter 6, we discuss the inevitability of the two largest economies in the world to become competitors of each other, intentionally or unintentionally. However, we also note that in many aspects, China still lags far behind the U.S. In Chapter 7, we examine the potential technological competition between China and the U.S., motivated by both economic and national security considerations. While China has been catching up rapidly on science and technology, there is still a significant gap between the two countries. In Chapter 8, we discuss how economic interdependence between China and the U.S. can be enhanced while simultaneously closing the trade gap, thus helping both countries to avoid the so-called "Thucydides Trap".

In Chapter 9, we consider long-term forces that underlie the economic relations between the two countries beyond the 2018 trade war. In this connection, we also consider how a "new type of major-power relation" between the two countries can help to keep the competition friendly and avert a war between them. Finally, the way forward for China-U.S. relations is discussed in Chapter 10.

Part I

Understanding the Trade War:
History, Facts and Potential Impacts

2. Historical Highlights of China-U.S. Relations

Relations between China and the U.S. first began with trade in the late 18th century. China, under the Qing Dynasty (1644–1912), and the U.S. formally recognised each other in 1844. The 1849 gold rush in Northern California attracted many Chinese miners from China. Thus, in China's southern province of Guangdong, from where most of the miners came, the U.S. is known as the "Gold Mountain".[1] The construction of the U.S. trans-continental railroad, completed in 1869, also employed many Chinese workers, some of whom also participated in the building of Stanford University later. Yung Wing[2], the first Chinese student known to graduate from a university in the U.S. (Yale College, Class of 1854), led the Chinese Educational Mission (1872–1881) of 120 young Chinese students[3] to the U.S., which unfortunately was eventually aborted.

In the 19th and the first half of the 20th centuries, the U.S. was the only major power without a colony, "concession" (leased territory) or sphere of influence in China. Every other major power—the U.K., France, Germany, Russia and even Japan—had administrative control or exclusive sphere of influence over some territories in China. The U.S. only advocated an "Open-Door" policy, proposed by John Hay, its Secretary of State, in 1899, which argued for equal access for all countries in trading with China and

---

1   The city of San Francisco is still referred to in Chinese as the "Old Gold Mountain" (舊金山).

2   In Putonghua pinyin, the name is phoneticised as Róng Hóng.

3   These were mostly young men in their early teens.

supported the territorial integrity of China. The relations between China and the U.S. were generally positive and cordial during this period.

However, the U.S. was a participant, along with Austria-Hungary, France, Germany, Italy, Japan, Russia and the U.K., in the Eight-Nation Alliance, which sent an international military expedition to Beijing to relieve the siege of the citizens of their respective nations by the "Boxers", a paramilitary martial arts group that had the support of the then Chinese government, in the summer of 1900. The Alliance defeated the Boxers as well as the Chinese Imperial Army, and the Empress Dowager Cixi, the de facto ruler of China at the time, had to flee from Beijing. The hostilities ended with the signing of the Boxer Protocol in 1901, which provided significant indemnities, known as the "Boxer Indemnity", for the Eight Nations, including the U.S.

Subsequently, both the government and the people of the U.S. contributed to and assisted in the development of China during the first half of the 20th century. For example, the U.S. eventually returned part of the funds from its share of the Boxer Indemnity to China. These funds were used to support a scholarship programme for Chinese students to study in the U.S. and to establish a preparatory school, Tsinghua Xuetang, in Beijing. Tsinghua Xuetang became the predecessor of Tsinghua University, one of the leading universities in China today. The Peking Union Medical College (PUMC), a leading medical school and hospital in Beijing, was jointly founded by American and British missionaries and the Chinese government in 1906. Subsequently, it received significant support from the Rockefeller Foundation beginning in 1915.

The Qing Dynasty was overthrown by the 1911 Revolution. The Republic of China was established in 1912, and was then recognised by the U.S. In 1917, China entered World War I on the side of the U.S., the U.K., France and others and sent a large number of workers to Europe to work on the front lines. However, the very unsatisfactory decisions of the Versailles Peace Conference, which favoured Japan at the expense of China, led to the May Fourth Movement, a series of large demonstrations and protests against the Chinese government and the old established order in China.

In 1937, the Sino-Japanese War (1937–1945) broke out in full. Before the U.S. declared war on Japan in the aftermath of Japan's surprise attack on Pearl Harbour, the volunteer American pilots, known as Flying Tigers, supported China in the war under the leadership of U.S. General Claire Chennault. After the U.S. entered World War II, U.S. General Joseph W. Stilwell was appointed the Commander-in-Chief of the China-Burma-India Theatre as well as the Chief of Staff to Generalissimo Chiang Kai-Shek, the war-time leader of China. General George C. Marshall, Jr., who later served as U.S. Secretary of State, tried to mediate between the Communists and the Nationalists in China between 1945 and 1947, but was not successful in preventing the Chinese Civil War that ensued.

In 1949, the Communists defeated the Nationalists in the Chinese Civil War and established the People's Republic of China. Before the outbreak of the Korean War (1950–1953), the U.S. maintained an official position of neutrality with regard to the two parties to the Chinese Civil war.[4] However, China's entry into the Korean War in the form of the (Chinese) People's Volunteer Army made China and the U.S. enemies. It also led to the imposition of a trade embargo against China by the U.S. Moreover, China supported North Vietnam in the Vietnam War[5] (1955–1975) whereas the U.S. fought on the side of South Vietnam. Nevertheless, China and the U.S. held intermittent ambassadorial-level talks between August 1955 and February 1970, first in Geneva and then in Warsaw. Yet the Sino-Soviet dispute, which began in the late 1950s and early 1960s, provided an opening for a Sino-U.S. détente. The secret visit by U.S. Secretary of State Henry Kissinger to China in 1971 led to a thaw in the relationship between the two countries. China was able to assume its seat in the United Nations Assembly and the Security Council with the tacit support of the U.S. later in 1971, and the trade embargo was lifted, except for strategic and defence-related goods. This was followed by the visit of U.S. President Richard Nixon to China in 1972, which made possible U.S.-China cooperation against the Soviet Union. The establishment of diplomatic relations between the

---

4   See, for example, United States Department of State (1949).
5   There were reports, never officially confirmed, that Chinese troops participated in the Vietnam War dressed as North Vietnamese soldiers.

Chart 2.1   Chinese Exports of Goods and Services to the World and to the U.S.
and Their Annual Rates of Growth (Chinese Official Data)

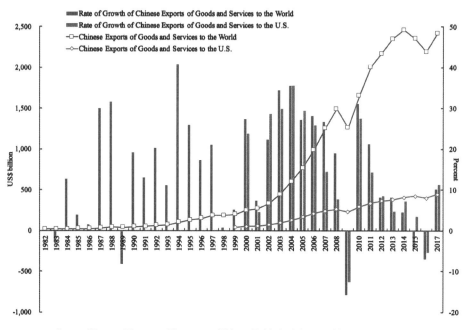

Source: National Bureau of Statistics of China. Published data on Chinese exports of services
to the U.S. prior to 1999 are not available.

People's Republic of China and the U.S. (during the administration of U.S. President James E. Carter), as well as China's decision to undertake economic reform and open its economy to the world, both in late 1978, created new opportunities for cooperation between the two nations. However, the Tiananmen Square incident on 4 June 1989, the fall of the Berlin Wall in November 1989 and the subsequent dissolution of the Soviet Union in 1991 profoundly altered the geo-political landscape of the world.

In the early 1990s, China and the U.S. had lengthy negotiations on the "most-favoured-nation" treatment for Chinese exports to the U.S. China was finally able to accede to the WTO in 2001, after which its exports to the world and to the U.S. expanded explosively for almost a whole decade (see Chart 2.1). It was this expansion of exports that enabled the massive transfer of the surplus labour force from the rural areas in China to the urban areas on China's coast to work in export-oriented, light manufacturing enterprises. This has been credited with lifting up to 800 million people out of poverty in China. Although the growth of Chinese exports to the world and to the U.S. has slowed significantly since 2012[6], the importance of the China's accession to the WTO, made possible with the consent and support of the U.S., to the subsequent economic success of China, should not be underestimated.

---

6   Data on China's exports of services to the U.S. prior to 1999 are not available. However, they are believed to be small. Data on China's exports of goods only are presented in Chart 4.9 below.

3. The Reality of the China-U.S. Trade Balance[1]

The statistical agencies of both the Chinese and the U.S. governments collect and publish statistics on their trade in goods and services with the world and with each other. However, their data on their bilateral trade, and in particular, on their bilateral trade balance, do not seem to agree. For example, in 2017, Chinese exports of goods to the U.S., according to the National Bureau of Statistics of China, were US$433.1 billion[2] on a "free on board" (f.o.b.) basis; however, according to the U.S. Census Bureau or the Bureau of Economic Analysis of the U.S. Department of Commerce, U.S. imports of goods from China were US$505.5 billion[3] on a "customs basis". There was a difference of 16.7 percent![4] It should therefore not be surprising that the official estimates of the bilateral trade balance can differ significantly between the two countries.

There are several reasons for these differences to arise. They include differences in the definitions, that is, the different conventions of measuring exports as f.o.b. or "free alongside ship" (f.a.s.), and imports as "cost, insurance and freight" (c.i.f.) or "customs basis"[5]; differences in the timing of the exports departing the country of origin and arriving at the country

---

1   This chapter is based on Xikang Chen, Lawrence J. Lau, Junjie Tang and Yanyan Xiong (2018).
2   See Table A3.4 in the appendix to this chapter.
3   See Table A3.3.
4   The typical difference between f.o.b. and c.i.f. valuations should be 10 percent.
5   That is, the value of the imports based on the assessment of the customs officer.

of destination[6]; differences in the treatment of indirect trade (that is, re-exports through a third country or region); and differences in the exchange rate(s) used in the conversion from the Chinese Renminbi to the U.S. Dollar (or vice versa). Transfer pricing is frequently used by exporters so that the profits can be taxed in a lower-tax-rate jurisdiction and this typically involves re-exporting through a third country or region. Intentional false declaration by importers in order to avoid or reduce customs duties is yet another possible reason for the discrepancies between the values of exports recorded by the exporting country and the value of imports recorded by the importing country.

In this chapter, we review and analyse the official statistics of both China and the U.S. on bilateral trade between them, with the intent of trying to reconcile their differences. We attempt to reconstruct estimates of China-U.S. trade and the trade balance, in terms of the gross value of the goods and services traded between the two countries, which hopefully will better reflect the reality of the situation. In addition, based on the reconstructed estimates of China-U.S. trade, we shall also estimate the China-U.S. trade balance in terms of the domestic value-added, that is, GDP generated by the exports of each country to the other.

The bilateral trade balance between two countries is generally not considered an important issue by most mainstream economists. It is the aggregate trade balance of a country with the rest of the world that really matters. However, there is also in many countries the latent mercantilist feeling that it is an advantage for a country to have a trade surplus, based on the simplistic idea that exports generate inbound revenue and create domestic jobs whereas imports generate outbound expenditure and destroy domestic jobs. Thus, the precise numerical magnitude of the bilateral trade balance can become a politically important and sensitive issue in the relation

---

6   In steady state, when the level of exports is stationary, the timing does not matter. However, when trade is either rising or falling reasonably rapidly, the timing might make a difference. Exports shipped in December from an origin country and arriving in January in the destination country will count as exports of the same year in the origin country but imports of the following year in the destination country, possibly leading to a discrepancy.

between two countries, as in the case of China and the U.S. It therefore behoves both China and the U.S. to have an accurate estimate of the value of their bilateral trade surplus or deficit. Moreover, any attempt on the part of both governments to close the trade gap requires a common understanding of its true nature and size.

International Trade between Two Countries Always Benefits Both

Before we begin, it is useful to explain why voluntary trade between two countries always benefits both in the aggregate. This is because with the possibility of trade, the choices open to the firms and households of each of the two countries are greatly expanded. The firms and households in both countries can have access to goods and services that were previously unavailable to them. If the two countries decide voluntarily to trade, they must both be better off, because they can always choose not to do so. If there is no gain for either of the trading-partner countries, no trade will take place. Thus, in the aggregate, the welfare of each of the two trading-partner countries must be improved with trade. International trade is therefore always win–win for both trading-partner countries, and this is totally independent of whether trade is balanced or which of the two countries has a bilateral trade surplus or deficit.

The set of production possibilities of an economy is the set of all possible combinations of goods and services that it can produce in a given period, such as a year. In Chart 3.1, the set of production possibilities of an economy with two goods, X1 and X2, is shown, shaded in blue. It contains all the possible combinations of the two goods that the economy is capable of producing. The solid blue line is the frontier of the set of production possibilities. An economy that is efficient always operates on the frontier of its set of production possibilities, because on the frontier, the production of good X1 cannot be increased without a decrease in the production of good X2, and vice versa; whereas in the interior of the set of production possibilities, the production of both goods can be simultaneously increased by simply moving towards the frontier. Moreover, the more of good X1 that

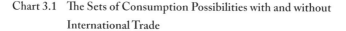

Chart 3.1   The Sets of Consumption Possibilities with and without
           International Trade

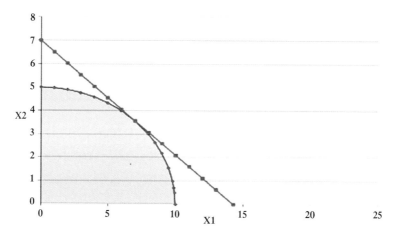

the economy has already been producing, the more of good X2 it has to give
up on the margin in order to produce an additional unit of good X1. (This
is the diminishing marginal rate of substitution, or convexity, assumption.)

In the absence of international trade, the set of consumption possibilities of an economy, that is, all the possible combinations of the two goods
that are available for the economy to consume, is precisely the same as its
set of production possibilities. The firms and households in the economy
can only consume what the economy is capable of producing. With international trade, the set of consumption possibilities of the economy can be
expanded even with the set of production possibilities remaining the same.
The straight red line in Chart 3.1 represents the international price line. Its
slope is the ratio at which a unit of good X2 can be exchanged for a unit of
good X1 on the world market. It is drawn at its point of tangency to the set
of production possibilities.[7]

With international trade, the set of consumption possibilities becomes
the triangle bounded by the straight red line and the vertical and horizontal
axes. To see this, suppose initially the economy operates at the point of

---

7   It is assumed that the economy is small and has no influence on international prices, so
     that it is a price-taker in the world market, and thus the price line is a straight line.

tangency of the set of production possibilities to the international price line, then by exporting part of the good X1 that it has produced and importing good X2 internationally, it can attain every other point on the red line to the left of the point of tangency. Similarly, by exporting part of the good X2 that it has produced and importing good X1 internationally, it can attain every other point on the red line to the right of the point of tangency. If every point on the red line can be achieved, then every point below the red line, which has the same quantity of X1 and a smaller quantity of X2, can also be achieved. Thus, every combination of goods X1 and X2 below and including the straight red line and bounded by the vertical and the horizontal axes are attainable with international trade. The set of consumption possibilities with international trade clearly contains the entire set of production possibilities (and the original set of consumption possibilities under autarky).

Thus, the economy must be better off because not only does it have all the previously available consumption possibilities to choose from, but it also has many more choices previously unavailable to it. The net gain in each of the trading-partner countries is therefore always positive in the aggregate.

However, international trade may create, within each country, both winners and losers. The benefits to an economy from international trade can be manifested in two principal ways. First, its exporters can produce more goods and export them, and thereby create more GDP, profits and employment for the economy. Second, its importers also benefit as the demands for imports generate revenues and profits for them as well as create additional employment; further, its consumers can enjoy more, cheaper and a greater variety of imported consumer goods, and its producers can enjoy more and cheaper imported inputs including equipment, energy, material and service inputs. Yet the occurrence of new international trade transactions will necessitate domestic adjustments in both trading-partner countries, as some domestic industries will expand while other domestic industries will contract. Imports can potentially disrupt domestic industries through their competition with domestically produced goods and the displacement of workers employed in these domestic industries. International trade can also change the relative prices between different goods in the economy; for example, increased exports can also create losers by bidding away domestic resources needed by other industries. Losers will be created in the domestic economy unless appropriate compensation and redistribution policies are adopted by the government. The free market on its own cannot compensate the losers from international trade. Only the government can redistribute the net gains, by taxing the winners and subsidising the losers, in the form of transitional assistance such as unemployment benefit, living allowances, retraining grant and early retirement subsidies, if it chooses to do so. But as demonstrated above, with voluntary international trade, there is always a net gain for each of the trading-partner countries in the aggregate, so that it should be possible for the government of each country to redistribute the gains so that no one loses.

Finally, the same argument above also shows that whenever a previously autarkic economy joins the world economy and begins to trade with other countries, such as the economic opening of China in 1978, total international trade of the entire world should increase. Moreover, the aggregate economic welfare of each country that participates in the world economy should also increase.

A Review of the Official Chinese and U.S. Statistics on Their Trade with the World

At the present time, the U.S. and China are respectively the largest and the second largest trading nations in the world. In Chart 3.2, the annual levels (respectively the red and blue lines) and rates of growth (respectively the red and blue columns) of the total international trade (including both goods and services) of China and the U.S., according to their respective official statistics, are presented (the underlying data are presented in Tables A3.1 and A3.2 in the appendix to this chapter). It shows that the U.S. has been the largest trading nation in the world for decades and still is today. However, it also shows that even though China is a relative latecomer to the world economy, it has also become a major trading nation, second only to the U.S. Chinese international trade increased rapidly beginning in the 1990s, and especially after China's accession to the WTO in 2001. Its rate of growth

Chart 3.2   Total Chinese and U.S. International Trade in Goods and Services and Their Annual Rates of Growth (Official Chinese and U.S. Statistics)

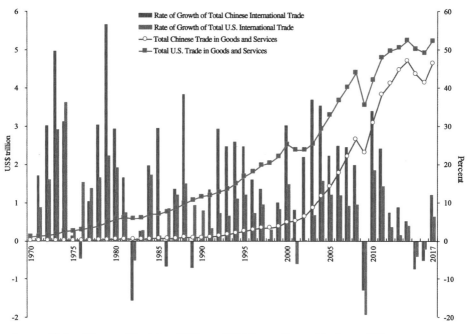

Sources: National Bureau of Statistics of China and U.S. Census Bureau. The data on U.S. international trade of goods and services are taken from the U.S. national income accounts.

was higher than that of the U.S. in every year since 1991. World trade itself took a significant hit during the global financial crisis of 2008–2009 but recovered relatively quickly. However, the growth of international trade has slowed down for both China and the U.S. since 2012.

It is worth pointing out that the conventions used by the Chinese and the U.S. statistical agencies in their respective measurements of exports and imports are not exactly the same, and hence the lines and columns for China and the U.S. in Chart 3.2 are not directly comparable. The U.S. measures exports of goods on an f.a.s. basis, that is, the value of the goods, including inland transportation, if any, before the goods are loaded on the vessel. Almost the entire rest of the world, including China as well as the IMF, measure exports of goods on an f.o.b. basis, that is, the value after the goods are loaded on the vessel, including the loading costs. For the same shipment, the f.o.b. valuation is typically assumed to be 1 percent higher than the f.a.s. valuation. The U.S. also measures imports of goods on a "customs basis", that is, based on the assessment of the customs officers. However, almost the entire rest of the world, including China as well as the IMF, measure imports of goods on a c.i.f. basis. The relationship between "customs basis" and c.i.f. basis is not entirely clear. Fortunately, the IMF publishes the trade statistics of all countries in the world with exports of goods valued f.o.b. and imports of goods valued c.i.f., including the U.S. Presumably this is based on data submitted by the official statistical agencies of every country, including the U.S. Thus, a comparison of the total U.S. exports of goods, f.a.s., as reported by the U.S. Census Bureau, with the total U.S. exports of goods, f.o.b., as reported by the IMF, should tell us the difference between the two methods of valuation. Similarly, a comparison of the total U.S. imports of goods, reported on a "customs basis" by the U.S. Census Bureau, with the total U.S. imports of goods, as reported on a c.i.f. basis by the IMF, should also tell us the difference between the two methods of valuation, if any. A comparison between the values of U.S. exports to China and U.S. imports from China, as separately reported by the U.S. and the IMF, will also throw light on the f.o.b.-f.a.s. ratio and the c.i.f.–customs basis ratio respectively. There is, of course, no valuation differences in the measurement of exports and imports of services.

In Tables 3.1 and 3.2, the official U.S. statistics of total exports and imports of goods to and from the world and China respectively are compared with those of the IMF. Table 3.1 reveals that for U.S. exports of goods only to the world, there seems to be no difference between f.a.s. and f.o.b. valuations.[8] However, for U.S. exports to China, the f.o.b. valuation is higher than the f.a.s. valuation as expected. The difference ranges between 0.3 and 2.3 percent, and follows a downward trend over time. We shall use the IMF data for U.S. exports f.o.b. in our further calculations.[9] Since China and the

---

8   We cannot explain why there is no difference between the f.a.s. and f.o.b. valuations for total U.S. exports to the world.

9   There are also slight differences in the IMF and the respective national treatments of certain items, for example, the exports and imports of gold bullion. However, it is believed that such differences are not large enough to make a material difference.

Table 3.1   A Comparison of the Official Export Statistics of the U.S. and the
              IMF (US$ million)

Year	U.S. Exports of Goods Only to the World (f.a.s.)	U.S. Exports of Goods Only to the World (f.o.b.)	Implied f.o.b.-f.a.s. Ratio	U.S. Exports of Goods Only to China (f.a.s.)	U.S. Exports of Goods Only to China (f.o.b.)	Implied f.o.b.-f.a.s. Ratio
1985		212,778		3,856	3,938	1.021
1986		227,158		3,106	3,176	1.023
1987		254,124		3,497	3,574	1.022
1988		322,427		5,022	5,121	1.020
1989	363,817	363,812	1.000	5,755	5,865	1.019
1990	393,610	393,592	1.000	4,806	4,903	1.020
1991	421,710	421,730	1.000	6,278	6,394	1.018
1992	448,164	448,164	1.000	7,419	7,548	1.018
1993	465,092	464,773	0.999	8,763	8,908	1.017
1994	512,627	512,627	1.000	9,282	9,432	1.016
1995	584,743	584,743	1.000	11,754	11,928	1.015
1996	625,072	625,073	1.000	11,993	12,169	1.015
1997	689,183	689,182	1.000	12,862	13,047	1.014
1998	682,138	682,138	1.000	14,241	14,437	1.014
1999	695,798	695,797	1.000	13,111	13,298	1.014
2000	781,918	781,918	1.000	16,185	16,396	1.013
2001	729,099	729,100	1.000	19,182	19,413	1.012
2002	693,101	693,103	1.000	22,128	22,375	1.011
2003	724,770	724,771	1.000	28,368	28,645	1.010
2004	814,873	814,875	1.000	34,428	34,833	1.012
2005	901,081	901,082	1.000	41,192	41,873	1.017
2006	1,025,967	1,025,967	1.000	53,673	54,812	1.021
2007	1,148,198	1,148,199	1.000	62,937	64,314	1.022
2008	1,287,442	1,287,442	1.000	69,733	71,346	1.023
2009	1,056,043	1,056,043	1.000	69,497	70,637	1.016
2010	1,278,493	1,278,495	1.000	91,911	93,059	1.012
2011	1,482,507	1,482,508	1.000	104,122	105,445	1.013
2012	1,545,820	1,545,821	1.000	110,517	111,855	1.012
2013	1,578,517	1,578,517	1.000	121,746	122,852	1.009
2014	1,621,874	1,621,874	1.000	123,657	124,729	1.009
2015	1,503,329	1,503,328	1.000	115,873	116,505	1.005
2016	1,451,022	1,451,024	1.000	115,546	115,942	1.003
2017	1,546,274	1,546,273	1.000	129,894	130,377	1.004

Sources: U.S. Census Bureau, U.S. Bureau of Economic Analysis and IMF.

Table 3.2   A Comparison of the Official Import Statistics of the U.S. and the
             IMF (US$ million)

Year	U.S. Imports of Goods Only from the World (customs basis)	U.S. Imports of Goods Only from the World (c.i.f.)	Implied c.i.f.– customs basis Ratio	U.S. Imports of Goods Only from China (customs basis)	U.S. Imports of Goods Only from China (c.i.f.)	Implied c.i.f.– customs basis Ratio
1985		352,463		3,862	4,224	1.094
1986		382,294		4,771	5,241	1.098
1987		424,443		6,294	6,910	1.098
1988		459,543		8,511	9,261	1.088
1989	473,217	492,922	1.042	11,990	12,901	1.076
1990	495,300	516,987	1.044	15,237	16,296	1.069
1991	488,440	508,363	1.041	18,969	20,305	1.070
1992	532,665	553,923	1.040	25,728	27,413	1.065
1993	580,658	603,438	1.039	31,540	33,513	1.063
1994	663,255	689,215	1.039	38,787	41,362	1.066
1995	743,542	770,852	1.037	45,543	48,521	1.065
1996	795,291	822,025	1.034	51,513	54,409	1.056
1997	869,704	899,020	1.034	62,558	65,832	1.052
1998	911,898	944,353	1.036	71,169	75,109	1.055
1999	1,024,617	1,059,435	1.034	81,788	86,481	1.057
2000	1,218,021	1,259,297	1.034	100,018	106,215	1.062
2001	1,140,999	1,179,177	1.033	102,278	109,392	1.070
2002	1,161,365	1,200,227	1.033	125,193	133,490	1.066
2003	1,257,121	1,303,050	1.037	152,436	163,255	1.071
2004	1,469,705	1,525,516	1.038	196,682	210,526	1.070
2005	1,673,454	1,735,061	1.037	243,470	259,838	1.067
2006	1,853,938	1,918,077	1.035	287,774	305,788	1.063
2007	1,956,961	2,020,403	1.032	321,443	340,118	1.058
2008	2,103,640	2,169,487	1.031	337,773	356,319	1.055
2009	1,559,625	1,605,296	1.029	296,374	309,558	1.044
2010	1,913,856	1,969,884	1.029	364,953	382,983	1.049
2011	2,207,955	2,266,024	1.026	399,371	399,371	1.000
2012	2,276,268	2,336,485	1.026	425,619	425,619	1.000
2013	2,267,988	2,328,507	1.027	440,430	440,434	1.000
2014	2,356,356	2,421,330	1.028	468,475	466,754	0.996
2015	2,248,810	2,315,889	1.030	483,202	481,881	0.997
2016	2,187,599	2,249,944	1.028	462,542	462,813	1.001
2017	2,341,964	2,408,476	1.028	505,470	505,597	1.000

Sources: U.S. Census Bureau and IMF.

IMF use the same measurement conventions for exports and imports, it is not necessary to compare China's data with the IMF data.

Table 3.2 reveals that for U.S. imports of goods only from the world and from China, the c.i.f. valuation seems to be higher that the "customs basis" valuation. The ratio of c.i.f. to "customs basis" is higher for China, reflecting perhaps the greater average shipping distance between the U.S. and China compared to the other major trading-partner countries of the U.S., such as Canada and Mexico. However, since 2011, there have been quite a few years for which the ratio is equal to 1.0, indicating no difference between c.i.f. and "customs basis".[10]

In Chart 3.3, the annual levels (respectively the red and blue lines) and rates of growth (respectively the red and blue columns) of the total international trade in goods only of China and the U.S., according to their respective official statistics, are presented.[11] It shows that China has been the largest trading nation in goods in the world since 2012.

In Chart 3.4, the annual levels (respectively the red and blue lines) and rates of growth (respectively the red and blue columns) of the total international trade in services of China and the U.S., according to their respective official statistics, are presented.[12] It shows that U.S. international trade in services far exceeds that of China. In fact, the U.S. has been and still is the largest trading nation in services in the world today.

In Chart 3.5, the annual levels (respectively the red and blue lines) of the total trade surplus or deficit in goods and services combined and separately of goods only and services only of China and the U.S. with the world, according to their respective official statistics, are presented.[13] It shows that China has been running a substantial trade surplus with the rest of the world since 1990 but the U.S. began to run a trade deficit in goods and services combined with the rest of the world since 1976, long before

---

10   We also cannot explain why there is no difference between the c.i.f. and "customs basis" valuations for U.S. exports to China for certain years.

11   The underlying data are also presented in Tables A3.1 and A3.2.

12   Ibid.

13   Ibid.

Chart 3.3   Total Chinese and U.S. International Trade in Goods Only and Their
            Annual Rates of Growth (Official Chinese and U.S. Statistics)

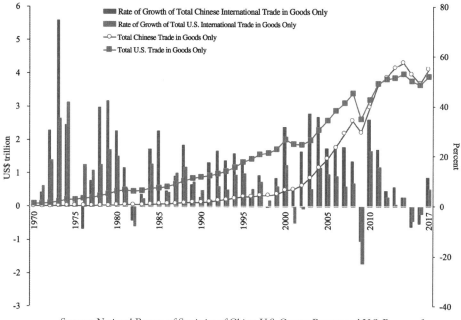

Sources: National Bureau of Statistics of China, U.S. Census Bureau and U.S. Bureau of
Economic Analysis.

China's opening to the world economy, and which has continued to grow. Moreover, the total U.S. trade deficit with the world, at US$540 billion in 2017, was much larger than China's total trade surplus of US$154 billion with the world. Thus, China's trade surplus with the world was less than 30 percent of the U.S. trade deficit. However, the U.S. has also been running a large trade surplus in services with the rest of the world. The U.S. trade surplus in services only was US$255 billion in 2017, also much larger than China's trade surplus in goods and services combined.

In Chart 3.6, the annual trade surplus or deficit in goods and services combined and separately of goods only and services only of China and the U.S. (respectively the red and blue lines) with the world, as a percent of their respective GDP, according to their respective official statistics, are

Chart 3.4   Total Chinese and U.S. International Trade in Services and Their
Annual Rates of Growth (Official Chinese and U.S. Statistics)

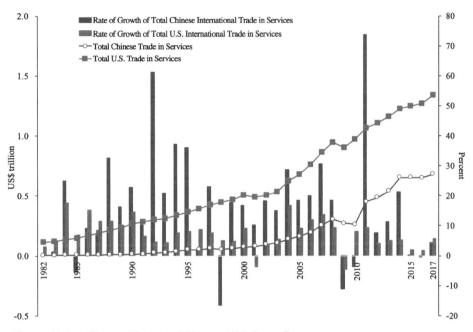

Sources: National Bureau of Statistics of China and U.S. Census Bureau.

presented. It shows that China's trade surplus with the world as a percentage of its GDP reached a peak of 7.3 percent in 2007 and has declined substantially since then to 1.3 percent in 2017. It also shows that the U.S. has been running a persistent trade deficit in goods and services vis-à-vis the world since 1976. It began with a deficit of 0.09 percent of GDP in 1976, which grew to 5.58 percent at its highest point in 2006. This reflects the investment-savings balance in the two countries—China saves more than it invests domestically, and the U.S. saves less than what it invests domestically. Recently the total U.S. trade deficit has stayed slightly below 3 percent of its GDP.

Chart 3.5   Chinese and U.S. Trade Surplus (Deficit) with the World in Goods
             and Services, Goods Only and Services Only
             (Official Chinese and U.S. Statistics)

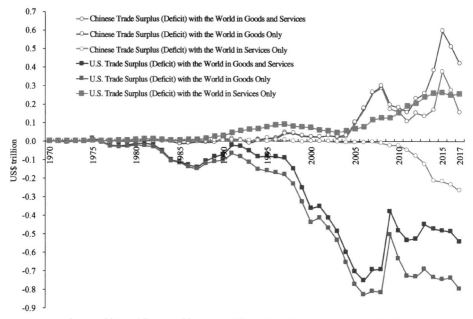

Sources: National Bureau of Statistics of China, U.S. Census Bureau and U.S. Bureau of
Economic Analysis.

A Review of the Official Chinese and U.S. Statistics of China-U.S. Trade

Trade between the U.S. and China has also grown by leaps and bounds since China began its economic reform and opening in 1978. In Chart 3.7, the U.S. exports and imports of goods and services combined, as well as its exports and imports of goods only, to and from China, and the corresponding bilateral trade balances, according to official U.S. statistics, are presented. In Table A3.3, the official U.S. statistics of exports of goods and services to and imports of goods and services from China are presented. Chart 3.7 shows that according to official U.S. statistics, in 2017, the U.S. had a trade deficit in goods of US$375.6 billion and a trade surplus in services of US$40.2

Chart 3.6 Chinese and U.S. Trade Surplus (Deficit) with the World in Goods and Services, Goods Only and Services Only as a Percent of GDP (Official Chinese and U.S. Statistics)

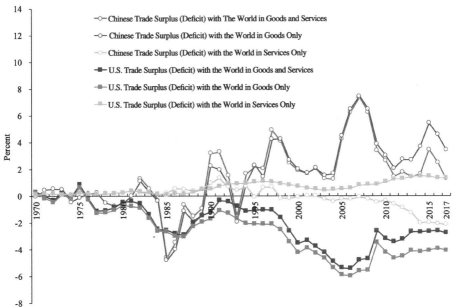

Sources: National Bureau of Statistics of China, U.S. Census Bureau and U.S. Bureau of Economic Analysis.

billion with China. Combining the trade in both goods and services, the U.S.-China trade deficit, according to official U.S. statistics, was US$335.4 billion in 2017.

In Chart 3.8, China's exports of goods and services and goods only to and imports of goods and services and goods only from the U.S., and the bilateral trade balances, according to official Chinese statistics, are presented. It shows that, according to official Chinese statistics, China had a surplus in trade in goods with the U.S. of US$278 billion with the U.S. and a deficit in trade in services with the U.S. of US$55 billion in 2017.[14] Combining

---

14   China does not regularly publish data on bilateral trade in services. The data on the China-U.S. trade in services are partly derived through interpolation and splicing. See Xikang Chen, Lawrence J. Lau, Junjie Tang and Yanyan Xiong (2018).

Chart 3.7   U.S. Exports and Imports of Goods and Services and Goods Only to and
           from China and the Bilateral Trade Balances (Official U.S. Statistics)

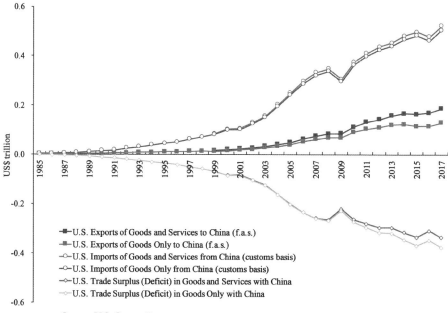

Source: U.S. Census Bureau.

the trade in both goods and services, the China-U.S. trade surplus was
US$223 billion, according to official Chinese statistics, much smaller than
the US$335 billion according to official U.S. statistics. In Table A3.4, the
official Chinese statistics on exports and imports of goods and services
to and from the U.S. are presented. Charts 3.7 and 3.8 both confirm the
historical facts of a very rapid growth in China-U.S. bilateral trade since the
early 1990s, especially after China's accession to the WTO in 2001, and the
emergence of a large bilateral trade surplus in favour of China.

In Chart 3.9, the annual levels of bilateral China-U.S. trade and the
implied trade balances according to Chinese and U.S. official statistics are
presented. It shows that there exist large differences between the Chinese
and the U.S. official estimates of their bilateral trade flows and trade balance.
According to official Chinese statistics, the U.S.-China trade deficit in 2017
for goods and services combined was US$223 billion; however, according to

Chart 3.8   Chinese Exports and Imports of Goods and Services and Goods
            Only to and from the U.S. and the Bilateral Trade Balances (Official
            Chinese Statistics)

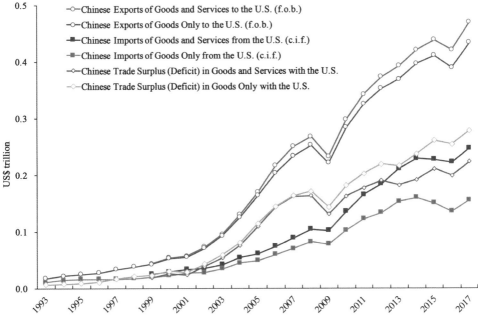

Source: National Bureau of Statistics of China. Chinese exports of services to the U.S. and
Chinese imports of services from the U.S. for the years 2007–2015 and 2017 are estimated by
Xikang Chen, Lawrence J. Lau, Junjie Tang and Yanyan Xiong (2018).

official U.S. statistics, the U.S.-China total trade deficit in 2017 was US$335
billion, a difference of more than 50 percent!

There are also large differences between the official statistics on bilateral trade in services of the two countries. For example, in 2016, the
U.S. recorded exports of services to China of US$55 billion whereas China
recorded imports of services from the U.S. of US$87 billion. China also
recorded exports of services to the U.S. of US$31 billion whereas the U.S.
recorded imports of services of only US$16 billion from China. Service
flows are more difficult to measure than goods flows because they do not
have to go through customs. Moreover, the standards of measurement may
differ significantly across countries. Some service flows, such as royalties and

Chart 3.9   The Levels of China-U.S. Bilateral Trade in Goods and Services and
the Bilateral Trade Balances (Official Chinese and U.S. Statistics)

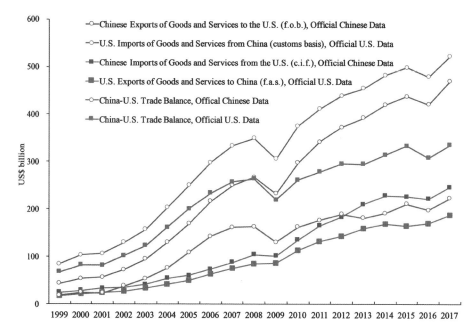

Sources: National Bureau of Statistics of China and U.S. Census Bureau.

license fee payments, payments for professional services, communications
and transportation costs, are relatively easy to track. Other service flows,
such as educational and tourism expenditures, are much more difficult. In
Chart 3.10, the annual levels of bilateral China-U.S. trade in services and
the implied trade balances according to Chinese and U.S. official statistics
respectively are presented. It shows the wide divergence between the Chinese and the U.S. official estimates of their bilateral trade flows and trade
balance in services. However, it is unmistakable that the U.S. has a large and
growing trade surplus vis-à-vis China in services since 2007.

Chart 3.10 The Levels of China-U.S. Bilateral Trade and Trade Balance in
Services (Official Chinese and U.S. Statistics)

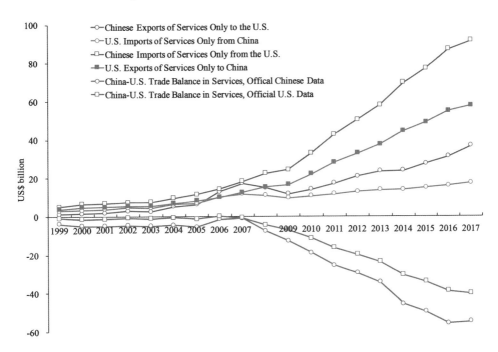

Note: See Xikang Chen, Lawrence J. Lau, Junjie Tang and Yanyan Xiong (2018).

A Reconciliation of the Official Chinese and U.S. Statistics on China-U.S. Trade

The analysis above shows that significant differences exist between official
Chinese and U.S. trade statistics on the magnitudes of the China-U.S. trade
balance in goods and services as well as separately in goods and in services.
These differences arise from a number of factors.[15] First, the long-estab-
lished international convention that exports of goods are measured on an
f.o.b. basis and imports on a c.i.f. basis[16], means that the value of imported

---

15   See, for example, the discussion in Kwok-Chiu Fung, Lawrence. J. Lau and Yanyan
      Xiong (October 2006).
16   The U.S. measures exports on an f.a.s. basis and imports on a "customs basis".

goods as measured by the importing nation is always different and almost always higher than the same goods as measured by the exporting nation as they leave its shores, since the measured value of imports includes not only the cost of the goods but also the costs of the insurance and freight. If two countries have exactly the same value of exports f.o.b. to each other, they will both show a measured trade deficit with each other in their bilateral trade balance. Thus, there is a "built-in" bias towards finding a bilateral deficit, as well as an overall deficit with the rest of the world. Since one country's exports must be another country's imports, total world exports should be exactly equal to total world imports. But it is not—total world imports are always greater than total world exports, because of the different conventions used in the measurement of exports and imports.

Thus, Chinese exports of goods to the U.S. according to official Chinese statistics are almost always less than U.S. imports of goods from China according to official U.S. statistics, and vice versa. We propose to rely solely on export data on an f.o.b. basis in the calculation of bilateral trade balances so as to avoid the built-in bias caused by the use of f.o.b. valuation for exports and c.i.f. valuation for imports. In any case, the costs of insurance and freight can and should be included in the trade in services.[17] Fortunately, even though the U.S. official statistics report U.S. exports on an f.a.s. basis, the U.S. also reports to the IMF on an f.o.b. basis, so we can use the IMF data on U.S. exports instead.

Second, Chinese exports of goods to the U.S. according to official Chinese statistics include only direct exports to the U.S. but not re-exports to the U.S. through Hong Kong, or for that matter through any third country or region, whereas U.S. imports of goods from China, according to official U.S. statistics, include Chinese re-exports through Hong Kong because the U.S. applies its rules of origin with regard to imports. Similarly, U.S. exports of goods to China, according to official U.S. statistics, do not include re-exports of U.S. goods to China through third countries and

---

17   In fact, insurance and freight may well be provided by third-country providers and not necessarily by the country exporting the goods.

regions. In addition, there may be re-exports through third countries that are not included in the data of the exporting country but included in the data of the importing country. And there may also be valuation problems due to transfer-pricing and customs duty avoidance. Thus, the values of the re-exports through Hong Kong have to be added back into the direct export data of both countries, converted to an f.o.b. Chinese or U.S. ports basis.[18]

Third, the increasingly important trade in services between China and the U.S. is often not included in the calculation of the trade balance, in part because of the unavailability of published data on bilateral trade in services.[19] The U.S. has a persistent, significant, positive and growing trade surplus in services with China. Thus, the inclusion of the trade in services will reduce the total U.S.-China bilateral trade deficit. Moreover, trade in services can be more reliably measured by the importing country than by the exporting country because the service providers in the exporting country have to be paid by the importing country, which means that the payments can be better tracked in the importing country. Thus, it is better to measure Chinese exports of services to the U.S. by the imports of services data of the U.S. and the U.S. exports of services to China by the imports of services data of China.

Professor Kwok-Chiu Fung of the University of California, Santa Cruz and I made the first attempt to reconcile the differences between official Chinese and U.S. statistics.[20] For the year 1995, the official U.S. estimate of the China-U.S. trade surplus of US$33.8 billion may be adjusted downwards to US$23.3 billion, a reduction of more than 30 percent. Former Chinese Premier Zhu Rongji actually used the analysis in Fung and Lau (1996, 1998) to show that the U.S.-China trade deficit was not as

---

18　In earlier studies on China-U.S. trade balance, Fung and Lau (1996, 1998) also take into account markups on re-exports through Hong Kong. It is believed that the markups are no longer important today.

19　There are published official U.S. data on the bilateral China-U.S. trade in services. However, such time-series are not available from China on a continuous basis. Xikang Chen, Lawrence J. Lau, Junjie Tang and Yanyan Xiong (2018) have attempted to estimate the bilateral trade in services based on occasional data released by China.

20　See Fung and Lau (1998).

large as the official U.S. data indicated. As we can see from our comparison of the official statistics of both countries above, these large discrepancies have persisted. In what follows, we shall attempt to reconstruct the bilateral trade statistics and reconcile the differences between the official statistics of China and the U.S. on their bilateral trade.

First, we standardise the measurement of the trade in goods of both countries in terms of exports on an f.o.b. basis, relying only on the data of the exporting country. The results are presented in Table 3.3. With this adjustment, our estimate of the U.S.-China trade deficit in goods for 2017 is US$303 billion, in-between the official U.S. estimate of US$376 billion and the official Chinese estimate of US$278 billion.

Second, we consider the inclusion of re-exports from Hong Kong— both re-exports of imported Chinese goods to the U.S. and imported U.S. goods to China. Data on re-exports are available from the Census and Statistics Department of Hong Kong on an f.o.b. Hong Kong basis. They need to be converted back to f.o.b. Chinese ports and f.o.b. U.S. ports respectively first before they can be added back to the Chinese and U.S. exports data. It is assumed that the Chinese exports f.o.b. Chinese ports are 100/105 of the Chinese re-exports f.o.b. Hong Kong, and that the U.S. exports f.o.b. U.S. ports are 100/110 of the U.S. re-exports f.o.b. Hong Kong.[21] The results are presented in Table 3.4. As a result of the adjustment for re-exports, our estimate of the U.S.-China trade deficit in goods for 2017 is increased to US$328 billion, still in-between the official U.S. estimate of US$376 billion and the official Chinese estimate of US$278 billion. This is because there are more re-exports to the U.S. than re-exports to China through Hong Kong.

Third, we consider the inclusion of the trade in services. As our previous discussion indicates, there are also significant differences between the official data of the two countries. We rely on the data of the importing country. The results are presented in Table 3.5. The inclusion of trade in ser-

---

21   The Chinese "discount" is smaller because the costs of insurance and freight for shipping Chinese goods to Hong Kong are lower than the costs of insurance and freight for shipping U.S. goods to Hong Kong. It is assumed that the former is 5 percent of the value of the re-exports and the latter is 10 percent of the value of the re-exports.

Table 3.3   Estimates of the U.S.-China Trade Deficit in Goods Only Based on Exporting Country f.o.b. Data (US$ million)

Year	Chinese Exports of Goods Only to the U.S. (f.o.b.)	U.S. Exports of Goods Only to China (f.o.b.)	U.S. Trade Surplus (Deficit) in Goods Only with China (Official U.S. Data)	Chinese Trade Surplus (Deficit) in Goods Only with the U.S. (Official Chinese Data)	China-U.S. Trade Balance, Goods Only (f.o.b.) (Based on Export Data)
1985		3,938	6		
1986		3,176	1,665		
1987		3,574	2,796		
1988		5,121	3,489		
1989		5,865	6,234		
1990		4,903	10,431		
1991		6,394	12,691		
1992		7,548	18,309		
1993	16,969	8,908	22,777	6,336	8,061
1994	21,408	9,432	29,505	7,431	11,975
1995	24,729	11,928	33,790	8,606	12,800
1996	26,708	12,169	39,520	10,529	14,539
1997	32,718	13,047	49,696	16,429	19,672
1998	37,965	14,437	56,927	20,968	23,528
1999	42,018	13,298	68,677	22,532	28,721
2000	52,142	16,396	83,833	29,777	35,746
2001	54,319	19,413	83,096	28,115	34,906
2002	69,959	22,375	103,065	42,732	47,584
2003	92,510	28,645	124,068	58,627	63,865
2004	124,973	34,833	162,254	80,321	90,140
2005	162,939	41,873	202,278	114,204	121,066
2006	203,516	54,812	234,101	144,293	148,704
2007	232,761	64,314	258,506	162,901	168,447
2008	252,327	71,346	268,040	170,829	180,981
2009	220,905	70,637	226,877	143,444	150,268
2010	283,375	93,059	273,042	181,314	190,316
2011	324,565	105,445	295,250	202,420	219,120
2012	352,000	111,855	315,102	219,122	240,145
2013	368,481	122,852	318,684	215,928	245,629
2014	396,147	124,729	344,818	236,960	271,418
2015	410,145	116,505	367,328	260,364	293,640
2016	389,113	115,942	346,996	253,988	273,171
2017	433,146	130,377	375,576	277,969	302,769

Sources: National Bureau of Statistics of China, U.S. Census Bureau and IMF.

Table 3.4   Estimates of the U.S.-China Trade Deficit Based on Exporting Country f.o.b. Data and Adjusted for Re-Exports (US$ million)

Year	Chinese Exports of Goods Only to the U.S. (f.o.b.)	U.S. Exports of Goods Only to China (f.o.b.)	Hong Kong Re-Exports of Imported Chinese Goods to the U.S. (f.o.b. Hong Kong)	Hong Kong Re-Exports of Imported Chinese Goods to the U.S. (f.o.b. Chinese ports)	Hong Kong Re-Exports of Imported U.S. Goods to China (f.o.b. Hong Kong)	Hong Kong Re-Exports of Imported U.S. Goods to China (f.o.b. U.S. ports)	Total Chinese Exports of Goods to the U.S. (f.o.b.)	Total U.S. Exports of Goods to China (f.o.b.)	China-U.S. Trade Balance, Goods Only (f.o.b.) (Based on Export Data Adjusted for Re-Exports)
1993	16,969	8,908	21,759	20,723	3,179	2,890	37,691	11,798	25,894
1994	21,408	9,432	25,333	24,127	3,710	3,372	45,534	12,805	32,730
1995	24,729	11,928	27,604	26,290	4,983	4,530	51,018	16,458	34,560
1996	26,708	12,169	29,224	27,833	5,868	5,335	54,541	17,504	37,037
1997	32,718	13,047	31,289	29,799	5,964	5,422	62,517	18,468	44,049
1998	37,965	14,437	30,894	29,423	5,288	4,808	67,388	19,245	48,144
1999	42,018	13,298	32,038	30,513	5,377	4,888	72,531	18,185	54,345
2000	52,142	16,396	36,484	34,747	6,113	5,557	86,889	21,953	64,936
2001	54,319	19,413	33,286	31,701	6,470	5,882	86,020	25,295	60,725
2002	69,959	22,375	34,337	32,702	6,206	5,641	102,662	28,017	74,645
2003	92,510	28,645	33,453	31,860	6,243	5,675	124,371	34,320	90,050
2004	124,973	34,833	35,534	33,842	5,789	5,262	158,816	40,095	118,721
2005	162,939	41,873	38,309	36,485	6,030	5,482	199,423	47,355	152,068
2006	203,516	54,812	40,127	38,216	6,524	5,931	241,733	60,743	180,990
2007	232,761	64,314	40,351	38,429	6,909	6,281	271,190	70,595	200,596
2008	252,327	71,346	39,768	37,874	8,099	7,363	290,201	78,709	211,492
2009	220,905	70,637	32,731	31,172	7,143	6,493	252,077	77,130	174,946
2010	283,375	93,059	37,678	35,884	8,630	7,845	319,259	100,904	218,355
2011	324,565	105,445	37,136	35,368	9,350	8,500	359,933	113,945	245,988
2012	352,000	111,855	38,397	36,569	9,496	8,633	388,569	120,488	268,080
2013	368,481	122,852	36,949	35,189	10,841	9,856	403,670	132,708	270,962
2014	396,147	124,729	37,774	35,975	11,374	10,340	432,123	135,069	297,054
2015	410,145	116,505	38,129	36,314	9,326	8,478	446,459	124,983	321,476
2016	389,113	115,942	35,678	33,979	9,430	8,573	423,092	124,515	298,577
2017	433,146	130,377	35,595	33,900	9,388	8,535	467,046	138,912	328,135

Sources: National Bureau of Statistics of China, U.S. Census Bureau, Census and Statistics Department of Hong Kong and IMF. The figures in red are derived in Xikang Chen, Lawrence J. Lau, Junjie Tang and Yanyan Xiong (2018).

vices, in which the U.S. has a significant trade surplus, results in an estimate of the U.S.-China trade deficit in goods and services combined for 2017 of US$254 billion[22], lower than both the official U.S. estimate of US$376 billion and the official Chinese estimate of US$278 billion for goods only. The potential of U.S. exports of services to China to continue to rise rapidly in the future is great unless it is affected by the trade war.

Table 3.5 shows that an "unbiased"[23] estimate of the China-U.S. trade balance in goods and services combined for the year 2017 would be US$254 billion. The U.S.-China trade deficit in goods, according to official U.S. data, was US$376 billion, compared to official Chinese data of US$278 billion. Using only exports of goods data, the U.S.-China trade deficit in goods only may be estimated as US$303 billion. After adding in re-exports through Hong Kong to both China and the U.S., the U.S.-China trade deficit in goods may be estimated as US$328 billion (see Table 3.4). If trade in services is included, based on imports of services data, the 2017 U.S.-China trade deficit can be estimated as US$254 billion, much lower than the often-quoted number of US$376 billion, but still a very large number nevertheless.

However, not fully included in the China-U.S. service trade figures are royalty and license-fee payments to third-country subsidiaries and affiliates of U.S. corporations such as Apple and Qualcomm. These are properly service revenues received by U.S. entities but attributed to third countries such as Ireland and the Netherlands. The precise values of these payments are not publicly available, but they are believed to be substantial. Thus, the true value of the U.S.-China trade deficit in goods and services, before adjustment to

---

22   In 2016, the official Chinese estimate for exports of services to the U.S. was US$31.2 billion compared to the official U.S. estimate of imports of services from China of US$16.0 billion. No published official data are available for the 2017 bilateral trade in services. However, if we assume that the official Chinese estimate on exports of services is more reliable and use it in our derivation, then our resulting estimate of the U.S.-China trade deficit would have been around US$270 billion.

23   We use the adjective "unbiased" because unlike the convention of measuring exports f.o.b. and imports c.i.f., which biases the trade balance towards deficits, our convention of using only data on exports f.o.b. is free of the bias.

Table 3.5   Estimates of the U.S.-China Trade Deficit in Goods and Services
Based on Exports of Goods (Including Re-Exports through Hong
Kong) and Imports of Services (US$ million)

Year	Chinese Exports of Goods Only to the U.S. (f.o.b.)	U.S. Exports of Goods Only to China (f.o.b.)	Hong Kong Re-Exports of Imported Chinese Goods to the U.S. (f.o.b. Chinese ports)	Hong Kong Re-Exports of Imported U.S. Goods to China (f.o.b. U.S. ports)	Total Chinese Exports of Goods to the U.S. (f.o.b.)	Total U.S. Exports of Goods to China (f.o.b.)	U.S. Imports of Services from China (U.S. data)	Chinese Imports of Services from the U.S. (Chinese data)	Reconstructed Trade Balance (Based on Exports of Goods and Imports of Services and Adjusted for Re-Exports)
1999	42,018	13,298	30,513	4,888	72,531	18,185	2,810	4,965	52,190
2000	52,142	16,396	34,747	5,557	86,889	21,953	3,297	6,450	61,783
2001	54,319	19,413	31,701	5,882	86,020	25,295	3,676	6,832	57,569
2002	69,959	22,375	32,702	5,641	102,662	28,017	4,607	7,462	71,790
2003	92,510	28,645	31,860	5,675	124,371	34,320	4,355	7,544	86,861
2004	124,973	34,833	33,842	5,262	158,816	40,095	6,308	9,624	115,404
2005	162,939	41,873	36,485	5,482	199,423	47,355	6,942	11,610	147,400
2006	203,516	54,812	38,216	5,931	241,733	60,743	10,177	14,400	176,767
2007	232,761	64,314	38,429	6,281	271,190	70,595	11,803	18,276	194,122
2008	252,327	71,346	37,874	7,363	290,201	78,709	10,946	22,466	199,972
2009	220,905	70,637	31,172	6,493	252,077	77,130	9,607	24,370	160,183
2010	283,375	93,059	35,884	7,845	319,259	100,904	10,637	33,048	195,944
2011	324,565	105,445	35,368	8,500	359,933	113,945	11,785	42,761	215,011
2012	352,000	111,855	36,569	8,633	388,569	120,488	13,015	50,441	230,654
2013	368,481	122,852	35,189	9,856	403,670	132,708	13,861	58,026	226,798
2014	396,147	124,729	35,975	10,340	432,123	135,069	13,968	69,626	241,396
2015	410,145	116,505	36,314	8,478	446,459	124,983	14,987	77,028	259,435
2016	389,113	115,942	33,979	8,573	423,092	124,515	16,032	86,900	227,709
2017	433,146	130,377	33,900	8,535	467,046	138,912	17,419	91,407	254,147

Sources: Table 3.4, Appendix Tables A3.3 and A3.4. The figures in red are derived in Xikang Chen, Lawrence J. Lau, Junjie Tang and Yanyan Xiong (2018).

a value-added basis, is probably no larger than US$250 billion a year, which is admittedly still a large number.

In Chart 3.11, we present three lines representing our reconstructed estimates of the U.S.-China trade deficit in goods and services combined, in goods only and in services only. It is clear that while the U.S. has a large trade deficit in goods with China, it also has a significant trade surplus in services with China. The overall U.S.-China trade deficit in goods and services combined in 2017, taking into account all the appropriate adjustments, may be estimated as US$254 billion.

Chart 3.11 Reconstructed China-U.S. Bilateral Trade Balance in Goods and
Services, Goods Only and Services Only (Official Chinese and U.S.
Statistics)

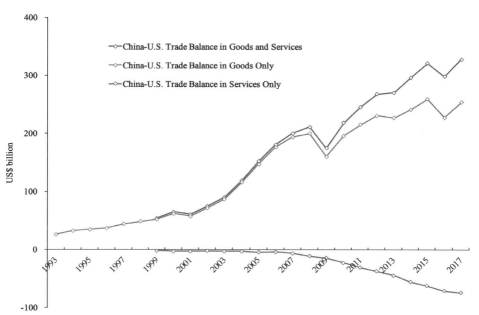

Sources: Appendix Tables A3.3 and A3.4. Published data on bilateral trade in services prior to 1999 are not available.

The China-U.S. Bilateral Trade Surplus in Terms of Domestic Value-Added

Thus far, the discussion of the U.S.-China trade deficit is on the basis of the gross value of exports. Ultimately, even the most accurately measured trade balance based on the gross value of exports of goods and services from each nation is not a reliable indicator of the relative benefit that each nation derives from bilateral trade. The real benefit that exports bring to an economy is the domestic value-added (GDP) and employment that it generates in the production of the goods exported, not its gross value. For exports of services, it is normally almost 100 percent domestic value-added—for example, for a foreign student studying in the U.S., his expenditure, including tuition and room and board, is considered to be U.S. exports of services, and is almost all domestic value-added.[24] Thus a more appropriate measure of the relative bilateral benefit is the trade balance measured in terms of value-added, and not gross value. The domestic value-added measures the GDP actually created by the production of the goods exported in the exporting country and can differ significantly from the gross value of the goods exported. For example, while the Apple iPhone is made in China, the domestic value-added in China is less than 5 percent of its gross export value.

Professor Xikang Chen of the Chinese Academy of Sciences and I with our collaborators introduced a new methodology to derive the domestic value-added and employment generated by Chinese exports to the U.S. and U.S. exports to China.[25] The direct domestic value-added content of Chinese exports of goods to the U.S. in 2015 was 24.8 percent on average[26], compared to the direct domestic value-added content of U.S. exports of goods to China of an average of 50.8 percent.[27] In Table 3.6, we derive the Chinese and U.S. exports of goods to each other in direct value-added terms using these factors, and calculate the resulting U.S.-China trade deficit in goods in terms of direct value added. Since the exports of services is almost all value-added, it can be simply added to the exports of goods in terms of value-added to obtain the U.S.-China trade deficit in goods and services combined in terms of direct value-added. It is found that the resulting U.S.-China trade deficit for 2017 is turned into a U.S.-China trade surplus of US$29 billion![28] While this may seem implausible at first, it is actually not difficult to understand. Consider the year 2017, when the Chinese exports to the U.S., including re-exports, f.o.b., was US$467 billion. Multiplying it by the direct domestic value-added coefficient (0.248), we obtain the estimated direct domestic value-added of US$116 billion. The U.S. exports

---

24   Of course, occasionally, the student may need to buy a foreign book.
25   See Lawrence J. Lau et. al. (October 2007). This article was subsequently translated into English and published as Lawrence J. Lau et. al. (February 2010). The former was awarded the Sun Yefang Prize in Economic Science in 2008 and the Peikang Chang Prize in Development Economics in 2009.
26   Xikang Chen and Huijuan Wang (2016), Tables 2.2 and 2.4.
27   Ibid., Tables 2.6 and 2.8.
28   See Xikang Chen, Lawrence J. Lau, Junjie Tang and Yanyan Xiong (2018).

Table 3.6   Reconstructed Estimate of the China-U.S. Trade Balance in Direct
Domestic Value-Added (US$ million)

Year	Chinese Exports of Goods Only to the U.S. (f.o.b.)	U.S. Exports of Goods Only to China (f.o.b.)	Direct Value-Added of Chinese Exports of Goods Only to the U.S.	Direct Value-Added of U.S. Exports of Goods Only to China	U.S.-China Trade Deficit in Goods Only (Direct Value-Added)	U.S. Imports of Services from China	Chinese Imports of Services from the U.S.	U.S.-China Trade Deficit in Services	U.S.-China Trade Deficit in Goods and Services (Direct Value-Added)
2013	403,670	132,708	100,110	67,416	-32,695	13,861	58,026	44,164	11,469
2014	432,123	135,069	107,166	68,615	-38,551	13,968	69,626	55,658	17,107
2015	446,459	124,983	110,722	63,491	-47,230	14,987	77,028	62,041	14,810
2016	423,092	124,515	104,927	63,254	-41,673	16,032	86,900	70,868	29,195
2017	467,046	138,912	115,827	70,567	-45,260	17,419	91,407	73,988	28,727

Sources: Table 3.4, Appendix Tables A3.3 and A3.4.

to China, including re-exports, f.o.b., was US$139 billion. Multiplying it by 0.508, we obtain the direct domestic value-added of US$71 billion. This leaves China with a trade surplus in direct domestic value-added of US$45 billion. However, the U.S. trade surplus in services in 2017, based on imports data, was US$74 billion. This is how it can result in the U.S. having an estimated trade surplus of US$29 billion with China in terms of direct domestic value-added.[29]

However, what we have just considered is the direct domestic value-added created in the economy from the production of the exported goods. The production of the domestic intermediate inputs used in the production of the exported goods also creates value-added in the economy—this is known as the second-round effect. The further production of the domestic intermediate inputs used in the production of the domestic intermediate inputs creates additional value-added, resulting in the third-, fourth- and successively higher-round effects. The total domestic value-added (GDP), taking into account all the rounds, may be estimated at 66 percent of the

29   If we assume that the Chinese estimate of exports of services to the U.S. is more reliable, then the surplus would be reduced by approximately US$15 billion, which would still leave an overall U.S. trade surplus of approximately US$14 billion in terms of direct domestic value-added.

Table 3.7   Reconstructed Estimate of the China-U.S. Trade Balance in Total Domestic Value-Added (US$ million)

Year	Chinese Exports of Goods Only to the U.S. (f.o.b.)	U.S. Exports of Goods Only to China (f.o.b.)	Total Value-Added of Chinese Exports of Goods Only to the U.S.	Total Value-Added of U.S. Exports of Goods Only to China	U.S.-China Trade Deficit in Goods Only (Total Value-Added)	U.S. Imports of Services from China	Chinese Imports of Services from the U.S.	U.S.-China Trade Deficit in Services	U.S.-China Trade Deficit in Goods and Services (Total Value-Added)
2013	403,670	132,708	266,422	117,712	148,711	13,861	58,026	44,164	104,546
2014	432,123	135,069	285,201	119,806	165,395	13,968	69,626	55,658	109,737
2015	446,459	124,983	294,663	110,860	183,803	14,987	77,028	62,041	121,762
2016	423,092	124,515	279,241	110,445	168,796	16,032	86,900	70,868	97,928
2017	467,046	138,912	308,251	123,215	185,036	17,419	91,407	73,988	111,048

Sources: Table 3.4, Appendix Tables A3.3 and A3.4.

value of Chinese exports to the U.S.[30], and 88.7 percent of the value of U.S. exports to China.[31] Using these factors, we can derive an estimate of the China-U.S. trade balance in terms of the total domestic value-added. This is done in Table 3.7, which shows that the U.S.-China trade deficit in goods and services combined in terms of total value-added may be estimated as US$111 billion.[32] US$111 billion is still a large number in China's favour but is much smaller than the often-mentioned US$376 billion based on gross value of exports of goods only. Moreover, it looks like a gap that is possible to narrow or even close in a few years' time if both China and the U.S. work together. The domestic value-added content of U.S. exports of goods to China is much higher than that of Chinese exports of goods to the U.S., especially agricultural and energy goods, which also have high demands in China (see discussions in Chapter 8).

---

30   See Xikang Chen and Huijuan Wang (2016), Table 2.4.
31   Ibid., Tables 2.6 and 2.8.
32   If we assume that the Chinese estimate of exports of services to the U.S. is more reliable, then the deficit would be increased by approximately US$15 billion, to US$125 billion in terms of total domestic value-added.

Chart 3.12 The U.S.-China Trade Deficit in Goods and Services, Goods Only
         and Services Only (Total Domestic Value-Added)

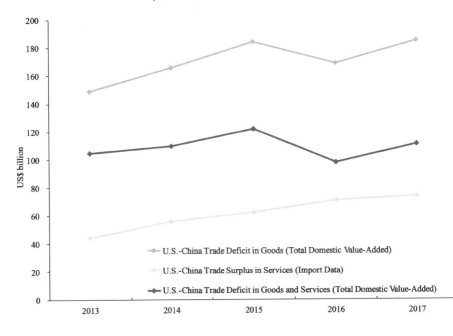

Sources: Tables 3.6 and 3.7.

Appendix

Table A3.1   Data on U.S. Exports, Imports, Total International Trade and Trade Surplus (Deficit) with the World (Official U.S. Statistics, US$ million)

Year	U.S. Exports of Goods and Services (f.a.s.)	U.S. Exports of Goods Only (f.a.s.)	U.S. Exports of Services Only	U.S. Imports of Goods and Services (customs basis)	U.S. Imports of Goods Only (customs basis)
1970	56,725	41,771	14,954	53,658	39,448
1971	59,940	42,870	17,070	60,037	44,973
1972	67,509	48,936	18,573	71,553	55,054
1973	90,895	71,069	19,825	88,003	69,542
1974	121,235	97,727	23,508	123,305	101,339
1975	132,998	106,412	26,586	118,689	95,964
1976	143,520	115,111	28,409	146,351	120,932
1977	153,149	121,819	31,330	176,845	148,230
1978	180,072	142,688	37,384	205,900	172,410
1979	222,385	179,105	43,280	245,348	206,956
1980	272,135	221,373	50,762	285,539	241,924
1981	296,325	235,886	60,438	308,916	260,738
1982	274,709	213,644	61,064	294,657	243,851
1983	268,658	205,311	63,347	319,535	265,494
1984	293,683	222,215	71,468	394,324	327,759
1985	294,567	218,489	76,078	406,182	334,590
1986	312,214	222,373	89,841	441,068	360,743
1987	354,525	255,900	98,625	495,768	404,587
1988	434,212	321,527	112,684	540,144	441,194
1989	493,354	363,817	129,537	576,453	473,217
1990	542,037	393,610	148,427	613,675	495,300
1991	586,155	421,710	164,445	607,962	488,440
1992	625,414	448,164	177,250	652,226	532,665
1993	651,008	465,092	185,916	704,433	580,658
1994	713,024	512,627	200,397	796,314	663,255
1995	803,923	584,743	219,180	884,938	743,542
1996	864,558	625,072	239,486	947,842	795,291
1997	945,274	689,183	256,091	1,035,636	869,704
1998	944,896	682,138	262,758	1,092,575	911,898
1999	967,140	695,798	271,342	1,217,508	1,024,617
2000	1,072,301	781,918	290,383	1,434,134	1,218,021
2001	1,003,422	729,099	274,323	1,354,462	1,140,999
2002	973,768	693,101	280,667	1,385,744	1,161,365
2003	1,014,744	724,770	289,974	1,499,342	1,257,121
2004	1,152,837	814,873	337,964	1,752,793	1,469,705
2005	1,274,088	901,081	373,007	1,977,903	1,673,454
2006	1,442,707	1,025,967	416,740	2,195,102	1,853,938
2007	1,636,596	1,148,198	488,398	2,329,534	1,956,961
2008	1,820,260	1,287,442	532,818	2,512,691	2,103,640
2009	1,568,763	1,056,043	512,720	1,946,428	1,559,625
2010	1,841,826	1,278,493	563,333	2,323,168	1,913,856
2011	2,110,289	1,482,507	627,782	2,643,714	2,207,955
2012	2,202,230	1,545,820	656,410	2,728,281	2,276,268
2013	2,279,972	1,578,517	701,455	2,729,075	2,267,988
2014	2,363,792	1,621,874	741,918	2,837,118	2,356,156
2015	2,258,638	1,503,329	755,309	2,740,776	2,248,810
2016	2,209,910	1,451,022	758,888	2,697,437	2,187,599
2017	2,343,964	1,546,274	797,690	2,884,434	2,341,964

Sources: U.S. Census Bureau and U.S. Bureau of Economic Analysis. The numbers in red have been estimated by applying a data-splicing technique to the export data reported in the U.S. national income accounts.

U.S. Imports of Services Only	Total U.S. Trade in Goods and Services	Official U.S. Trade Surplus (Deficit) in Goods and Services	Official U.S. Trade Surplus (Deficit) in Goods Only	Official U.S. Trade Surplus (Deficit) in Services Only
14,210	110,383	3,067	2,323	744
15,064	119,977	-97	-2,103	2,006
16,500	139,063	-4,044	-6,118	2,074
18,461	178,898	2,892	1,528	1,364
21,967	244,540	-2,071	-3,612	1,541
22,726	251,687	14,308	10,448	3,860
25,419	289,872	-2,831	-5,821	2,990
28,615	329,994	-23,697	-26,411	2,714
33,490	385,972	-25,828	-29,722	3,894
38,392	467,733	-22,963	-27,851	4,888
43,615	557,674	-13,404	-20,551	7,147
48,178	605,241	-12,591	-24,852	12,261
50,806	569,366	-19,949	-30,207	10,258
54,041	588,193	-50,878	-60,183	9,305
66,565	688,007	-100,640	-105,543	4,903
71,592	700,749	-111,614	-116,101	4,487
80,325	753,282	-128,853	-138,369	9,516
91,181	850,293	-141,243	-148,687	7,444
98,950	974,356	-105,932	-119,667	13,734
103,237	1,069,807	-83,099	-109,400	26,300
118,375	1,155,712	-71,638	-101,690	30,052
119,522	1,194,117	-21,807	-66,730	44,923
119,561	1,277,640	-26,812	-84,501	57,689
123,775	1,355,441	-53,425	-115,566	62,141
133,059	1,509,338	-83,290	-150,628	67,338
141,396	1,688,861	-81,015	-158,799	77,784
152,551	1,812,400	-83,284	-170,219	86,935
165,932	1,980,910	-90,362	-180,521	90,159
180,677	2,037,471	-147,679	-229,760	82,081
192,891	2,184,648	-250,368	-328,819	78,451
216,113	2,506,435	-361,833	-436,103	74,270
213,463	2,357,884	-351,040	-411,900	60,860
224,379	2,359,512	-411,976	-468,264	56,288
242,221	2,514,086	-484,598	-532,351	47,753
283,088	2,905,630	-599,956	-654,832	54,876
304,449	3,251,991	-703,815	-772,373	68,558
341,164	3,637,809	-752,395	-827,971	75,576
372,573	3,966,130	-692,938	-808,763	115,825
409,051	4,332,951	-692,431	-816,198	123,767
386,803	3,515,191	-377,665	-503,582	125,917
409,312	4,164,994	-481,342	-635,363	154,021
435,759	4,754,003	-533,425	-725,448	192,023
452,013	4,930,511	-526,051	-730,448	204,397
461,087	5,009,047	-449,103	-689,471	240,368
480,762	5,200,910	-473,326	-734,482	261,156
491,966	4,999,414	-482,138	-745,481	263,343
509,838	4,907,347	-487,527	-736,577	249,050
542,470	5,228,398	-540,470	-795,690	255,220

Table A3.2   Data on Chinese Exports, Imports, Total International Trade and
              Trade Surplus (Deficit) with the World
              (Official Chinese Statistics, US$ million)

Year	Chinese Exports of Goods and Services (f.o.b.)	Chinese Exports of Goods Only (f.o.b.)	Chinese Exports of Services	Chinese Imports of Goods and Services (c.i.f.)	Chinese Imports of Goods Only (c.i.f.)
1970		2,260			2,330
1971		2,640			2,200
1972		3,440			2,860
1973		5,820			5,160
1974		6,950			7,620
1975		7,260			7,490
1976		6,850			6,580
1977		7,590			7,210
1978		9,750			10,890
1979		13,660			15,670
1980		18,120			20,020
1981		22,007			22,015
1982	24,991	22,321	2,670	21,309	19,285
1983	24,992	22,226	2,766	23,384	21,390
1984	29,229	26,139	3,090	30,267	27,410
1985	30,448	27,350	3,098	44,775	42,252
1986	34,803	30,942	3,861	45,180	42,904
1987	43,518	39,437	4,081	45,701	43,216
1988	52,615	47,516	5,099	58,872	55,268
1989	58,739	52,538	6,201	63,050	59,140
1990	70,156	62,091	8,065	57,697	53,345
1991	81,391	71,843	9,548	67,912	63,791
1992	97,519	84,940	12,579	90,019	80,585
1993	106,327	91,744	14,583	115,995	103,959
1994	141,203	121,006	20,197	131,914	115,615
1995	173,199	148,780	24,419	157,306	132,084
1996	179,029	151,048	27,981	161,418	138,833
1997	217,029	182,792	34,237	170,338	142,370
1998	208,764	183,712	25,052	167,079	140,237
1999	224,301	194,931	29,370	197,352	165,699
2000	284,233	249,203	35,030	261,258	225,094
2001	305,273	266,098	39,175	282,825	243,553
2002	371,823	325,596	46,227	341,700	295,170
2003	489,537	438,228	51,309	468,072	412,760
2004	657,808	593,326	64,482	633,952	561,229
2005	840,422	761,953	78,469	743,924	659,953
2006	1,063,049	968,978	94,071	892,299	791,461
2007	1,345,507	1,220,060	125,447	1,085,241	956,115
2008	1,576,036	1,430,693	145,343	1,288,959	1,132,562
2009	1,324,175	1,201,612	122,563	1,151,902	1,005,923
2010	1,695,286	1,577,754	117,532	1,537,181	1,396,247
2011	2,099,428	1,898,381	201,047	1,991,328	1,743,484
2012	2,250,290	2,048,714	201,576	2,099,705	1,818,405
2013	2,416,010	2,209,004	207,006	2,280,597	1,949,989
2014	2,561,433	2,342,293	219,141	2,392,118	1,959,235
2015	2,490,867	2,273,468	217,399	2,115,284	1,679,564
2016	2,306,035	2,097,631	208,404	2,029,476	1,587,926
2017	2,469,802	2,263,349	206,453	2,315,663	1,843,793

Source: National Bureau of Statistics of China.

Chinese Imports of Services	Total Chinese Trade in Goods and Services	Official Chinese Trade Surplus (Deficit) In Goods and Services	Official Chinese Trade Surplus (Deficit) In Goods Only	Official Chinese Trade Surplus (Deficit) In Services Only
			-70	
			440	
			580	
			660	
			-670	
			-230	
			270	
			380	
			-1,140	
			-2,010	
			-1,900	
			-8	
2,024	46,300	3,682	3,036	646
1,994	48,376	1,608	836	772
2,857	59,496	-1,038	-1,271	233
2,523	75,223	-14,327	-14,902	575
2,276	79,983	-10,377	-11,962	1,585
2,485	89,219	-2,183	-3,779	1,596
3,604	111,487	-6,257	-7,752	1,495
3,910	121,789	-4,311	-6,602	2,291
4,352	127,853	12,459	8,746	3,713
4,121	149,303	13,479	8,052	5,427
9,434	187,538	7,500	4,355	3,145
12,036	222,322	-9,668	-12,215	2,547
16,299	273,117	9,289	5,391	3,898
25,222	330,505	15,893	16,696	-803
22,585	340,447	17,611	12,215	5,396
27,968	387,367	46,691	40,422	6,269
26,842	375,843	41,685	43,475	-1,790
31,653	421,653	26,950	29,232	-2,282
36,164	545,491	22,975	24,109	-1,134
39,272	588,099	22,448	22,545	-97
46,530	713,523	30,123	30,426	-303
55,312	957,608	21,465	25,468	-4,003
72,723	1,291,760	23,857	32,097	-8,240
83,971	1,584,345	96,498	102,000	-5,502
100,838	1,955,348	170,750	177,517	-6,767
129,126	2,430,747	260,266	263,945	-3,679
156,397	2,864,995	287,078	298,131	-11,054
145,979	2,476,078	172,273	195,689	-23,416
140,934	3,232,467	158,105	181,507	-23,402
247,844	4,090,756	108,101	154,898	-46,797
281,300	4,349,995	150,584	230,309	-79,725
330,608	4,696,607	135,413	259,015	-123,602
432,883	4,953,551	169,316	383,058	-213,742
435,719	4,606,151	375,583	593,904	-218,320
441,550	4,335,511	276,559	509,705	-233,146
471,870	4,785,466	154,139	419,556	-265,417

Table A3.3   U.S. Exports and Imports of Goods and Services to and from China and the Bilateral Trade Surplus or Deficit (Official U.S. Statistics, US$ million)

Year	U.S. Exports of Goods and Services to China (f.a.s.)	U.S. Imports of Goods and Services from China (customs basis)	U.S. Trade Surplus (Deficit) in Goods and Services with China	U.S. Exports of Goods Only to China (f.a.s.)
1985				3,856
1986				3,106
1987				3,497
1988				5,022
1989				5,755
1990				4,806
1991				6,278
1992				7,419
1993				8,763
1994				9,282
1995				11,754
1996				11,993
1997				12,862
1998				14,241
1999	16,784	84,598	−67,814	13,111
2000	20,888	103,315	−82,427	16,185
2001	24,148	105,954	−81,806	19,182
2002	27,525	129,800	−102,275	22,128
2003	33,821	156,791	−122,969	28,368
2004	41,293	202,990	−161,697	34,428
2005	49,389	250,412	−201,023	41,192
2006	63,720	297,951	−234,231	53,673
2007	75,523	333,246	−257,723	62,937
2008	85,030	348,718	−263,688	69,733
2009	86,017	305,981	−219,964	69,497
2010	113,942	375,590	−261,647	91,911
2011	132,228	411,156	−278,928	104,122
2012	143,372	438,634	−295,262	110,517
2013	159,252	454,291	−295,039	121,746
2014	168,214	482,443	−314,229	123,657
2015	164,894	498,189	−333,294	115,873
2016	170,485	478,574	−308,089	115,546
2017	187,522	522,889	−335,367	129,894

Sources: U.S. Census Bureau and U.S. Bureau of Economic Analysis. Numbers in red have been estimated by Xikang Chen, Lawrence J. Lau, Junjie Tang and Yanyan Xiong (2018).

U.S. Imports of Goods Only from China (customs basis)	U.S. Trade Surplus (Deficit) in Goods Only with China	U.S. Exports of Services Only to China	U.S. Imports of Services Only from China	U.S. Trade Surplus (Deficit) in Services with China
3,862	-6			
4,771	-1,665			
6,294	-2,796			
8,511	-3,489			
11,990	-6,234			
15,237	-10,431			
18,969	-12,691			
25,728	-18,309			
31,540	-22,777			
38,787	-29,505			
45,543	-33,790			
51,513	-39,520			
62,558	-49,696			
71,169	-56,927			
81,788	-68,677	3,672	2,810	863
100,018	-83,833	4,703	3,297	1,406
102,278	-83,096	4,966	3,676	1,290
125,193	-103,065	5,398	4,607	790
152,436	-124,068	5,454	4,355	1,099
196,682	-162,254	6,865	6,308	557
243,470	-202,278	8,197	6,942	1,255
287,774	-234,101	10,047	10,177	-130
321,443	-258,506	12,587	11,803	783
337,773	-268,040	15,297	10,946	4,351
296,374	-226,877	16,520	9,607	6,913
364,953	-273,042	22,031	10,637	11,394
399,371	-295,250	28,107	11,785	16,322
425,619	-315,102	32,855	13,015	19,840
440,430	-318,684	37,506	13,861	23,645
468,475	-344,818	44,556	13,968	30,589
483,202	-367,328	49,021	14,987	34,034
462,542	-346,996	54,939	16,032	38,907
505,470	-375,576	57,628	17,419	40,209

Table A3.4   Chinese Exports and Imports of Goods and Services to and from
            the U.S. and the Bilateral Trade Surplus or Deficit
            (Official Chinese Statistics, US$ million)

Year	Chinese Exports of Goods and Services to the U.S. (f.o.b.)	Chinese Imports of Goods and Services from the U.S. (c.i.f.)	Chinese Trade Surplus (Deficit) in Goods and Services with the U.S.	Chinese Exports of Goods Only to the U.S. (f.o.b.)
1993				16,969
1994				21,408
1995				24,729
1996				26,708
1997				32,718
1998				37,965
1999	43,110	24,451	18,659	42,018
2000	53,627	28,814	24,813	52,142
2001	56,150	33,036	23,115	54,319
2002	72,788	34,690	38,099	69,959
2003	95,048	41,427	53,621	92,510
2004	130,152	54,277	75,876	124,973
2005	169,167	60,345	108,822	162,939
2006	216,524	73,623	142,901	203,516
2007	250,065	88,137	161,928	232,761
2008	267,292	103,964	163,328	252,327
2009	232,547	101,831	130,716	220,905
2010	297,538	135,108	162,430	283,375
2011	341,816	164,905	176,911	324,565
2012	372,885	183,319	189,566	352,000
2013	392,060	210,578	181,482	368,481
2014	420,075	228,813	191,262	396,147
2015	437,548	226,809	210,739	410,145
2016	420,313	222,024	198,288	389,113
2017	469,750	246,584	223,167	433,146

Sources: National Bureau of Statistics of China, Ministry of Finance of China, U.S. Census Bureau and U.S. Bureau of Economic Analysis. The numbers in red have been estimated by Xikang Chen, Lawrence J. Lau, Junjie Tang and Yanyan Xiong (2018).

Chinese Imports of Goods Only from the U.S. (c.i.f.)	Chinese Trade Surplus (Deficit) in Goods Only with the U.S.	Chinese Exports of Services Only to the U.S.	Chinese Imports of Services Only from the U.S.	Chinese Trade Surplus (Deficit) in Services Only with the U.S.
10,633	6,336			
13,977	7,431			
16,123	8,606			
16,179	10,529			
16,290	16,429			
16,997	20,968			
19,486	22,532	1,092	4,965	-3,873
22,365	29,777	1,485	6,450	-4,964
26,204	28,115	1,831	6,832	-5,001
27,228	42,732	2,829	7,462	-4,633
33,883	58,627	2,538	7,544	-5,006
44,653	80,321	5,179	9,624	-4,445
48,735	114,204	6,228	11,610	-5,382
59,223	144,293	13,008	14,400	-1,393
69,861	162,901	17,304	18,276	-973
81,498	170,829	14,965	22,466	-7,501
77,461	143,444	11,642	24,370	-12,728
102,060	181,314	14,163	33,048	-18,885
122,144	202,420	17,252	42,761	-25,510
132,878	219,122	20,885	50,441	-29,556
152,552	215,928	23,579	58,026	-34,447
159,187	236,960	23,928	69,626	-45,698
149,781	260,364	27,403	77,028	-49,625
135,124	253,988	31,200	86,900	-55,700
155,177	277,969	36,604	91,407	-54,803

4. How Serious Are the Impacts?

The proximate cause of the current China-U.S. trade war is the large and persistent U.S.-China trade deficit in goods and services. The U.S.-China bilateral trade deficit was considered by the U.S. to be the result of unfair trade practices on the part of China. There are other U.S. economic grievances not directly related to trade as well, which will be discussed in Chapter 9. However, as pointed out in Chapter 3, there are significant differences in the official Chinese and U.S. estimates of the magnitude of the bilateral trade deficit itself. For 2017, the U.S. estimate of the trade deficit for goods only is US$376 billion, whereas China's estimate is only US$278 billion. As discussed in Chapter 3, the large discrepancy is due to many factors, such as differences in the valuation of exports and imports; differences in the treatment of re-exports through third countries and regions; and the inclusion or exclusion of trade in services, in which the U.S. enjoys a large annual surplus currently on the order of US$50 billion. After making all the appropriate adjustments, a more accurate estimate of the U.S.-China trade deficit in terms of gross value is US$254 billion—still a very large number.[1]

U.S. President Donald Trump wishes to reduce the U.S.-China trade deficit by US$100 billion. To accomplish this objective, he proposed imposing tariffs on up to US$250 billion worth of U.S. imports from China[2] (and

---

[1]   See the analysis in Xikang Chen, Lawrence J. Lau, Junjie Tang and Yanyan Xiong (2018).

[2]   The U.S. tariffs were imposed on Chinese imports in three separate rounds: a first on US$34 billion in July 2018, a second on US$16 billion in August 2018 and a third on US$200 billion in September 2018. Imports of consumer goods such as cell phones, garments and shoes are at the time of publication not subject to U.S. tariffs.

if necessary, on an additional US$267 billion worth of U.S. imports from China, thus practically covering all imports from China). Whether this can be done in a manner consistent with the WTO rules is not so clear, and China, like the European Union and other countries subject to new U.S. tariffs, have filed complaints with the WTO. However, these complaints are unlikely to resolve the disputes. Predictably, China retaliated with new tariffs on China's imports from the U.S. totalling US$110 billion[3], at various rates but mostly at 10 percent. Under the new tariffs, China's exports to the U.S. will most certainly fall, as will U.S. exports to China. However, just as increased voluntary trade between two trading-partner countries raises the aggregate welfare in both countries, an involuntary decrease in the trade between them lowers their aggregate welfare. It will thus be lose-lose for both China and the U.S.

Also discussed in Chapter 3 is an alternative method of measuring the bilateral trade surplus or deficit, namely in terms of the domestic value-added that the respective exports generate in the exporting country. The domestic value-added content of a good to be exported is the GDP generated by its manufacture, relative to its export value, which represents its real contribution to the domestic economy. For example, the Apple iPhone is assembled in China with components, parts and technology from all over the world. The export value of an iPhone is approximately US$500.[4] The domestic value-added of the iPhone, including that of all the domestic intermediate inputs used such as electricity, may be estimated at no more than US$20. Thus, the domestic value-added content is 4 percent (20 / 500). The average domestic value-added content of China's exports to the U.S. is approximately 25 percent.[5] The average domestic value-added content of

---

3   China's retaliatory tariffs were also imposed on U.S. imports in three separate batches: a first on US$34 billion in July 2018, a second on US$16 billion in August 2018 and a third on US$60 billion in September 2018. Approximately US$40 billion of U.S. imports, including large aircrafts, integrated circuits and semiconductors are at the time of publication not subject to Chinese tariffs.

4   This is the wholesale value, not the retail value.

5   Xikang Chen and Wang Huijuan (2016), Tables 2.2 and 2.4.

U.S. exports to China is approximately 50 percent[6], a ratio of two to one compared to the China's value-added content. As derived in Chapter 3, the U.S.-China trade deficit in goods and services, measured in terms of total domestic value-added content, may be estimated at US$111 billion in 2017.[7] This contrasts with the official U.S. estimate for the trade deficit in goods only of US$376 billion in gross-value terms.

However, US$111 billion is still a large number. An efficient and fruitful way to close this trade gap is for China to import from the U.S. additional goods that it needs but that have close to 100 percent U.S. domestic value-added content, such as oil and gas, agricultural commodities (such as meat and grains) and services, so that an additional US$150 billion worth of exports to China in gross-value terms from the U.S. would suffice.[8] The U.S. definitely has the capacity to increase its supply of these goods, and China has high and rising demands for these goods, so that such an increase in the trade between the two countries should be mutually beneficial. It is also completely feasible, but will take some time to develop and implement.[9]

The Immediate Impacts on China's Financial Markets

The immediate impact of the current trade war was psychological and fell mostly on China's financial markets. As a result of the trade war, uncertainty has increased worldwide. Expectations have turned negative. Confidence of firms and households has slipped. Consumption and investment have been partially put on hold.

Stock markets abhor uncertainty, and any uncertainty will lead to a decline. China's stock markets—Shanghai and Shenzhen, and even Hong Kong—have taken a direct hit from the start of the trade war (see Chart 4.1). The Shenzhen Stock Exchange has seen its average stock price decline by almost 25 percent since the beginning of 2018. Similarly, the average

---

6   Ibid., Tables 2.6 and 2.8.
7   See Xikang Chen, Lawrence J. Lau, Junjie Tang and Yanyan Xiong (2018).
8   See Xikang Chen and Huijuan Wang (2016), Tables 2.6 and 2.8.
9   See Lawrence J. Lau (June 2018), pp. 1850014-1–1850014-13.

Chart 4.1　China, Hong Kong and U.S. Stock Market Indexes
(January to October 2018, 1 January 2018 = 100)

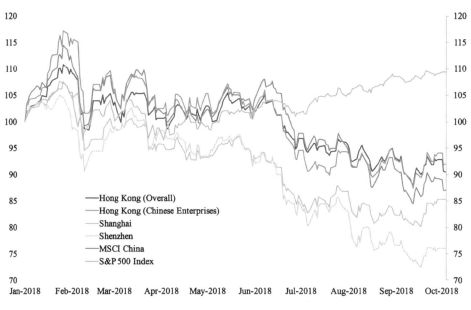

Source: Bloomberg.

price level of the Shanghai Stock Exchange has declined 15 percent. The MSCI China Index has declined 13 percent. Hong Kong overall has declined almost 10 percent, but mainland Chinese enterprises listed there have declined by somewhat less. In contrast, the S&P 500 Index has gained approximately 10 percent since the beginning of 2018. However, not all of the declines in China's stock markets can or should be attributed to the trade war. The actual and expected increases in the rate of interest in the U.S. by the U.S. Federal Reserve Board also had a role in the falling prices of assets worldwide and devaluing currencies vis-à-vis the U.S. Dollar in emerging and developing economies.[10]

However, the performance of the Shanghai and Shenzhen stock mar-

---

10　However, this does not explain why the S&P 500 Index kept hitting new highs—this is perhaps another round of "irrational exuberance".

kets is not a reliable barometer of the state of the Chinese economy. Rather, it is a measure of the degree of "irrational exuberance", to use a phrase coined by Dr. Alan Greenspan, the former Chairman of the U.S. Federal Reserve Board, or the opposite, "irrational gloom". This is because the mainland China's stock exchanges are dominated by individual investors, most of whom are only looking for quick profits through frequent trading. The average holding period of individual Chinese common stock investors is less than 20 trading days and that of institutional investors is between 30 and 40 trading days.[11] It does not help that most publicly listed Chinese enterprises pay little or no cash dividends. Since the trade war looks like it will last for a while, most mainland Chinese investors have elected to bail out and stay on the sidelines for now.

Similarly, the Renminbi exchange rate has also been negatively affected, but in part because of the actual and expected increases in the U.S. rate of interest. In Chart 4.2, an index of the Renminbi central parity rate, the rate set by the People's Bank of China (the central bank of China) at the beginning of each daily trading session of the onshore Renminbi, is compared to the China Foreign Exchange Trade System (CFETS) Index, an index of the changes in the value of a Chinese trade-weighted basket of foreign currencies[12], for the period since 2015.[13] While there was wide divergence between the two indexes at the beginning, they began to move in tandem with each other in the second half of 2017. More recently, while the Renminbi has devalued vis-à-vis the super-strong U.S. Dollar by approximately 9 percent since the end of January 2018, the average absolute deviation of the central parity rate from the CFETS Index has not widened beyond 1.7 percent (see Chart 4.3).

---

11   This is according to a report by the Capital Market Research Institute of the Shanghai Stock Exchange based on the transactions of all Chinese investors in 2016.

12   The U.S. Dollar had a weight of 26.4 percent before 2017. On 1 January 2017, the weights of the different currencies were adjusted in accordance with changes in the trade shares of the respective countries and regions. The U.S. Dollar currently has a weight of 22.4 percent. See the appendix to this chapter, Table A4.1.

13   Note that the offshore Renminbi exchange rates may be different from the onshore Renminbi exchange rates because capital controls still exist in China.

Chart 4.2   The Renminbi Central Parity Exchange Rate and the CFETS Index
           Since 2015 (31 December 2014 = 100)

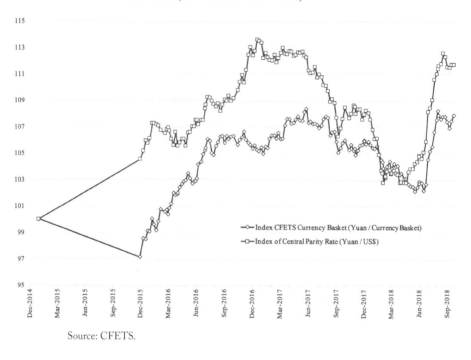

Source: CFETS.

Chart 4.3, which compares the movements of the Renminbi central parity rate and the CFETS Index since year-end 2017, shows that the central parity rate has devalued approximately 5 percent with respect to the U.S. Dollar (and 9 percent since the start of the trade war at the end of January 2018), in part also because of the actual and expected increases in the U.S. rate of interest, quite apart from the trade war. However, relative to the CFETS Index, the central parity rate has only devalued by 2.2 percent. A useful way of looking at the CFETS Index is that it measures the average (trade-weighted) change of the exchange rates of the currencies of China's trading-partner countries and regions relative to the Renminbi. So, if the percentage change of the Renminbi central parity rate is the same as that of the CFETS Index, it means that the Renminbi exchange rate is unchanged relative to the weighted average of the currencies of China's trading-partner countries, even though the Renminbi may have appreciated or devalued vis-

Chart 4.3   The Renminbi Central Parity Exchange Rate and the CFETS Index
(29 December 2017 = 100)

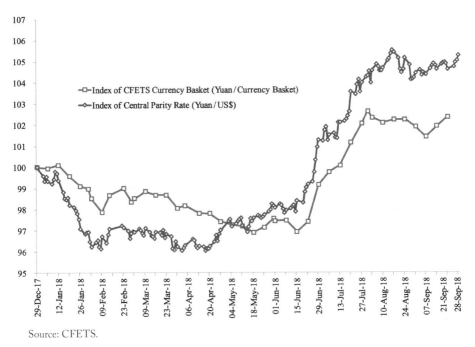

Source: CFETS.

à-vis a specific currency such as the U.S. Dollar. Actually, there is no compelling reason for the Renminbi to follow the U.S. Dollar lockstep, which
implies that the Renminbi will appreciate or devalue with respect to other
currencies precisely as the U.S. Dollar. When the U.S. Dollar is super-strong,
for the Renminbi to follow the U.S. Dollar effectively amounts to China's
exporters raising their prices to the importers of all other countries, which
does not necessarily make sense. If the Renminbi exchange rate follows
the CFETS Index, it is equivalent to keeping the Renminbi exchange rate
approximately constant for the average trading-partner country of China.

Another implication of the Renminbi exchange rate following the
CFETS Index is that the average purchasing power of the Renminbi overseas
will be preserved, that is, kept approximately constant. If the U.S. Dollar is
super-strong, U.S. goods will become more expensive, but the goods of other
countries will become cheaper, so that the Chinese consumers of imported

goods will on average be no worse off. Moreover, by following the CFETS Index, the Renminbi exchange rate will have a lower volatility than the U.S. Dollar exchange rate because Renminbi will move, in general, in the same direction as the U.S. Dollar but by a smaller amount. This means that when the U.S. Dollar appreciates with respect to other currencies, the Renminbi will devalue relative to the U.S. Dollar, and when the U.S. Dollar devalues with respect to other currencies, the Renminbi will appreciate relative to the U.S. Dollar. The Renminbi exchange rate will be less volatile than the U.S. Dollar exchange rate from the viewpoint of a third-country currency.

In assessing whether the Renminbi has devalued or appreciated, the focus should be placed on the spread between the central parity rate (on-shore rate) and the CFETS Index, and not just on the Chinese Yuan[14]–U.S. Dollar exchange rate. A super-strong U.S. Dollar can create turmoil in the foreign exchange markets of emerging and developing economies, as it has recently done in Argentina, India, Indonesia and Turkey. And when there is turmoil in the world for any reason, there will be an almost universal flight to the U.S. Dollar, the only major safe-haven currency. In the process, the U.S. Dollar will be strengthened and all the other currencies weakened. The Renminbi is no exception.

Despite widespread expectations that the Renminbi will be devalued significantly in response to the trade war, it is actually quite unlikely. The new U.S. tariff rate on China's exports of goods of 25 percent (after 1 January 2019) is prohibitively high relative to the profit margins of China's exporters and a moderate devaluation of the Renminbi accomplishes nothing except to make the Renminbi less desirable domestically and internationally as a medium of exchange and a store of value. For a large economy such as China's, with a relatively low degree of export dependence (see Charts 4.7 and 4.8 below), devaluation is never a useful strategy. It is also not necessary for the Renminbi to devalue. China's current account will remain in balance, even if China's exports to the U.S. decline by one half.[15] China's wage rate

---

14   The Yuan is a currency unit of the Renminbi.
15   See the discussion below.

in the private sector is still downwardly flexible, so economic adjustments can occur without having to tinker with the exchange rate. It is in China's interests to maintain a relatively stable Renminbi exchange rate so that its own citizens will continue to want to hold the Renminbi as a store of value. It is also the only way for the internationalisation of the Renminbi to eventually become a reality.

The people who will really be affected immediately by the new U.S. tariffs are the actual U.S. users of Chinese goods, consumers as well as producers, because they are the ones who will have to pay higher prices as a result of the new tariffs. Since China's imports arriving at U.S. ports have already been paid for by the U.S. importers, the cost of the tariffs will have to be passed on to the actual users in the U.S. to the greatest extent possible, or absorbed by the importers if their profit margins allow them to do so. However, the Office of the U.S. Trade Representative has announced that exemptions from the new tariffs for one year may be granted to U.S. importers upon application on a product-by-product basis. At the same time, it has also been reported that very few exemptions have been approved, so it is really not clear how things will end up at this time. The new tariffs have also kicked in on China's side, although there is no similar exemption for China's importers of U.S. goods. In this situation, China has simply been reacting to the U.S. moves, in a reciprocal but measured manner.

The Real Impacts on China's Economy

The new U.S. tariffs range in rate for the first batch of US$34 billion of China's imports into the U.S., and are 25 percent ad valorem for the second batch of US$16 billion and 10 percent for the third batch of US$200 billion (to be raised to 25 percent on 1 January 2019). While U.S. imports from China that have been already ordered will not be affected, and that in the short term the tariffs may even cause Chinese (and U.S.) exporters to accelerate their shipments to beat the expected imposition or increase of tariffs[16], the new tariffs will have an impact on the placement of future orders. A tariff rate of 25 percent will prove to be prohibitive for most of the goods imported from China, as neither China's exporters nor the U.S. importers have the kind of profit margins that can allow them to absorb the cost of these tariffs. Moreover, while alternative sources of supplies may not be immediately available, they can certainly be developed, given some lead time. Thus, the new U.S. tariffs, if fully implemented, will effectively lead to an almost complete halt of China's exports to the U.S. of goods that are subject to them, resulting in a potential reduction of U.S. imports of goods from China of up to US$250 billion on an "arrival valuation" or equivalently "cost, insurance and freight" (c.i.f.) basis. This translates to a reduction of China's exports to the U.S. of approximately US$225 billion on a "departure valuation" or equivalently "free on board" (f.o.b.) basis.[17] What will be the real impacts of such a reduction in exports on China's economy?

First of all, China, as a large continental economy with a huge domestic market, like the U.S., has a relatively low export dependence, and has always been relatively immune to external disturbances. During the past two decades, the rates of growth of China's exports and imports have fluctuated like those of all other Asian economies, large and small. Chart 4.4 presents the quarterly rates of growth of exports of selected Asian economies and Chart 4.5 presents the quarterly rates of growth of imports of the same selected Asian economies. The red lines in both charts, representing China's quarterly rates of growth of exports and imports respectively, fluctuate like those of all the other Asian economies. However, the quarterly rate of growth of China's real GDP, represented by a red line in Chart 4.6, has remained positive and relatively stable compared to those of all the other Asian economies, including Japan.

Moreover, China's dependence on exports has been declining over the past decade. The value of China's exports of goods and services to the world as a share of China's GDP fell from a peak of 35.3 percent in 2006 to 19.8

16   In fact, for the first ten months of 2018, China's exports to the U.S. rose 13.3 percent year-on-year and U.S. exports to China rose 8.5 percent year-on-year.
17   The reduction of U.S. imports from China of US$250 billion on a c.i.f. basis translates to approximately US$227 billion (250 × 10 / 11) on an f.o.b., Chinese ports, basis. We shall use the rounded-off number of US$225 billion.

Chart 4.4   Quarterly Rates of Growth of Exports of Goods—Selected Asian
Economies (Year-on-Year)

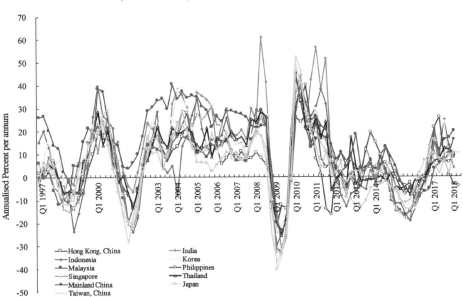

Source: IMF, *International Financial Statistics*.

Chart 4.5   Quarterly Rates of Growth of Imports of Goods—Selected Asian
Economies (Year-on-Year)

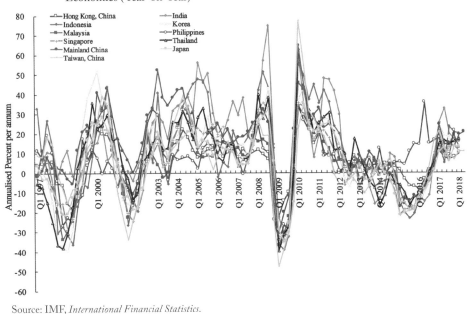

Source: IMF, *International Financial Statistics*.

Chart 4.6   Quarterly Rates of Growth of Real GDP—Selected Asian Economies (Year-on-Year)

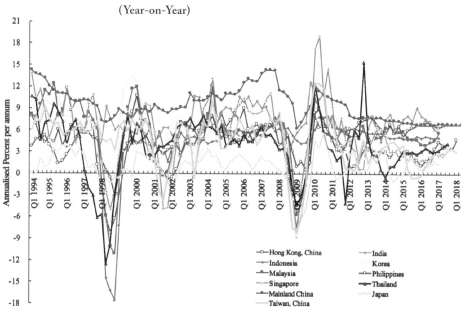

Source: IMF, *International Financial Statistics.*

percent in 2017, whereas the share of exports of goods alone fell from a peak of 31.5 percent to 18.1 percent of China's GDP in 2017 (see Chart 4.7). Similarly, the share of exports of goods and services to the U.S. in China's GDP also fell by more than half, from a peak of 7.6 percent in 2006 to 3.5 percent in 2017. For goods alone, at its peak the share stood at 7.2 percent and fell to 3.4 percent of China's GDP in 2017 (see Chart 4.8).

During this same period, the rates of growth of China's exports of goods to the world and to the U.S. (represented by the red and blue columns repectively in Chart 4.9) have also declined significantly. China's exports of goods to the world grew at an average annual rate of 22.6 percent in the decade 1998–2007, but slowed to only 7.9 percent in the following decade (2008–2017), in part because of the 2008–2009 global financial crisis and the subsequent European sovereign debt crisis. Similarly, exports to the U.S. grew at 22 percent per annum in the decade 1998–2007 but slowed to less than 7 percent per annum in the most recent decade. The most important engine of China's economic growth today is no longer exports but rather

Chart 4.7   China's Exports of Goods and Services and Goods Only as a Percent of China's GDP

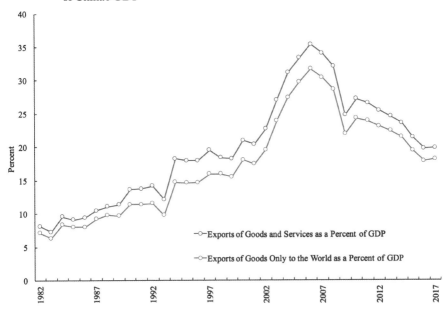

Source: State Administration of Foreign Exchange, China.

domestic demand, driven by its household consumption (especially that of the rapidly growing middle class), infrastructural investments, and public goods consumption such as environmental preservation, protection and restoration, education, health care and elderly care.

China's total exports of goods to the U.S. in 2017, on an f.o.b. basis, was US$433 billion according to the National Bureau of Statistics of China, or 3.4 percent of China's GDP in 2017.[18] At present, new U.S. tariffs are levied on US$250 billion worth of U.S. imports of goods from China. This is approximately equivalent to US$225 billion of China's exports of goods to

---

18   This is not the place to discuss or reconcile the discrepancy between Chinese and U.S. official data. However, if we add 10 percent to c.i.f. adjustment to the reported China's exports to the U.S. f.o.b. of US$430 billion, U.S. imports from China would amount to US$473 billion, which is not that far apart from the U.S. official data on imports of goods from China in 2017 of US$506 billion. The remaining discrepancy can be mostly attributed to re-exports through a third country or region like Hong Kong.

Chart 4.8   China's Exports of Goods and Services and Exports of Goods Only to the U.S. as a Percent of China's GDP

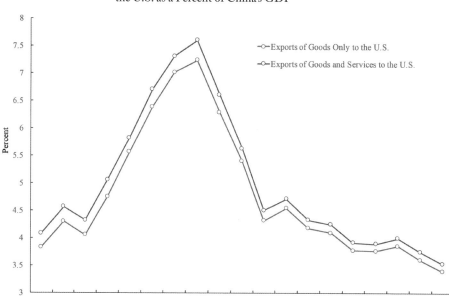

Sources: National Bureau of Statistics of China and U.S. Bureau of Economic Analysis.

the U.S. on an f.o.b. basis, or approximately half of the China's total exports of goods to the U.S. in 2017.[19] Assuming that half of all China's exports of goods to the U.S. will be halted because of the prohibitive new tariffs, China's total exports of goods to the world, which were US$2.28 trillion in 2017 according to China's official statistics, will fall by 9.9 percent. As a comparison, in the aftermath of the collapse of Lehman Brothers in 2008, China's total exports of goods actually declined by 16 percent in 2009, and China's economy still managed to grow 8.7 percent in real terms that year.

Of course, if the new tariffs turn out not to be completely prohibitive of U.S. imports from China, the decline in China's exports may be less.

---

19   Strictly speaking, half of US$430 billion is US$215 billion. However, it is well known that Chinese official data on exports do not include re-exports through third countries or regions such as Hong Kong, so US$225 billion may be a reasonable estimate of one half of China's exports of goods to the U.S. on an f.o.b. basis. See footnote 17 above.

Chart 4.9   The Rates of Growth of China's Exports of Goods to the World and to the U.S.

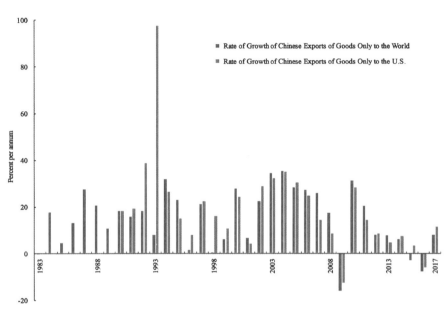

Source: National Bureau of Statistics of China.

The exact magnitude of the decline will depend on, among other things, the price elasticity of U.S. demand for China's exports, the value of which in turn depends on the export prices of other potential supplier countries and regions. If the price elasticity is unity (that is, a one-percent increase in the price results in a one-percent decline in the quantity demanded), then a 25-percent increase in the price, caused by the new U.S. tariffs, will result in a 25-percent decline in the quantity of China's exports, rather than a hundred percent, so that the decline in China's exports to the U.S. may be estimated at only a quarter of what we have assumed here. However, we believe that the great majority of China's exports to the U.S. subject to the new U.S. tariffs has ready sources of substitute supplies in other countries and regions. Neither China's exporters nor U.S. importers, with the possible exception of firms such as Apple Inc., have the kind of profit margins or market power that can enable them to absorb a 25-percent increase in cost. Moreover, one cannot entirely rule out the possibility that the tariff rate may be raised further if there is no truce in the trade war. Thus, most U.S. importers will be looking for alternative suppliers from other countries. Even if ultimately not all China's exports to the U.S. subject to the new U.S. tariffs will be halted, the decline will be large and significant, and our assumption of a total halt may be taken to be that for a conservative, worst-case scenario.

What would be the real impacts of such a fall in China's exports due to the new U.S. tariffs on China's real GDP? As China's total exports of goods to the U.S. was 3.4 percent of China's GDP in 2017, the decline of one half of China's exports of goods to the U.S. would amount to only 1.7 percent of GDP. Moreover, the direct domestic value-added content of China's exports is quite low—averaging 25.5 percent in the aggregate, and slightly lower for exports to the U.S., at 24.8 percent, in 2015.[20] This means that every U.S. Dollar of China's exports to the U.S. generates less than 25 U.S. cents of China's GDP.[21] In contrast, the direct domestic value-added content of U.S. exports of goods to China may be estimated at 50.8 percent in 2015, slightly more than twice the domestic value-added content of China's exports to the U.S.[22] Thus, the maximum loss in China's GDP in the first instance, assuming that half of the exports to the U.S. is completely halted, may be estimated at 0.43 percent (1.7 × 0.25), a tolerable level, especially for an economy growing at an average annual real rate of 6.5 percent and with a per capita GDP of US$9,137 in 2017, which is way above the subsistence level.

Thus, even if all China's exports to the U.S. subject to the new tariffs are halted and in addition are not re-directed elsewhere, the initial reduction in the domestic value-added (GDP) caused directly is less than half a percent. In the subsequent period, the reductions in the intermediate input demands of China's economy caused by the reduction of exports will cause further reductions in the intermediate input demands, accompanied by further reductions in the domestic value-added. This is the indirect second-round

20   Xikang Chen and Wang Huijuan (2016), Tables 2.2 and 2.4.
21   While the domestic value-added content of China's exports may have risen since 2015, the increase is not believed to be significant.
22   Xikang Chen and Wang Huijuan (2016), Tables 2.6 and 2.8.

effect. These further reductions in the intermediate input demands will in turn cause further reductions of the intermediate input demands as well as domestic value-added (GDP), as the third-, fourth- and higher-round effects kick in, but with the effects becoming successively smaller with each higher round. The total effect on domestic value-added (GDP), taking into account all the rounds, may be estimated at 66 percent of the value of the reduced exports.[23] This implies ultimately a maximum total loss in China's GDP of 1.12 percent (1.7 × 0.66). In absolute terms, this amounts to US$137 billion in 2017 prices compared to China's GDP of US$12.2 trillion in 2017. A reduction of 1.12 percent from an expected annual growth rate of 6.5 percent leaves 5.38 percent, still a very respectable rate compared to the average of 3.7 percent for the world as a whole in 2018, as forecast recently by the IMF.

Even with a fall in China's exports of goods to the U.S. by one half, amounting to 1.7 percent of China's GDP, China's total trade in goods and services, which had a surplus with the world equal to 1.71 percent of GDP in 2017, will still remain in balance, without taking into account any potential reduction of China's imports from the U.S. (see Chart 4.10). China's trade surplus in goods and services with the U.S. was 1.86 percent of China's GDP in 2017. If U.S. imports from China are reduced by a half, that is, by 1.71 percent of China's GDP, China's trade with the U.S. will still remain in a slight surplus. Thus, there should be little pressure for the Renminbi to devalue as a result of the new U.S. tariffs from balance of payments considerations. In fact, it is probably in the best interests of China's economy to maintain a relatively stable Renminbi exchange rate.

There is a possibility that the scope of the U.S. tariffs may be expanded to cover all U.S. imports from China, in which case the full negative economic impact will be doubled to 2.24 percent of China's GDP at a maximum, but still leaving China's economy an expected rate of growth in excess of 4 percent. If this happens, it is likely that the Chinese government will undertake a targeted economic stimulus programme to increase aggregate demand on

---

23   Ibid., Table 2.4.

Chart 4.10   China's Trade Surplus in Goods and Services with the World and the
             U.S. as a Percent of China's GDP

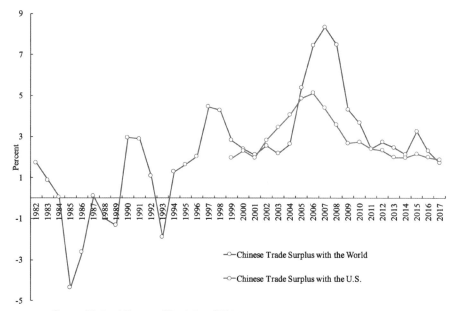

Source: National Bureau of Statistics of China.

the margin to mitigate the negative impacts of the trade war. It will probably
be focused on investments in basic infrastructure, research and development
(R&D), provision of public goods such as environmental preservation,
protection and restoration—blue skies, green mountains and turquoise
waters—and education, health care and elderly care, rather than fixed investment in the manufacturing or housing sectors. With all the existing
excess production capacities in China, supply should not be a constraint—if
there is demand, there will be supply.

    In the longer run, assuming that the tariffs continue on both sides, the
U.S. importers will begin to replace China's imports by imports from other
Asian countries such as Vietnam, Cambodia and Bangladesh, and eventually perhaps even North Korea. That is why the new tariffs against China
may not lower the overall U.S. trade deficit with the world. The history of
the U.S. apparel trade provides an interesting example. Between 1989 and
2017, the share of Hong Kong, Taiwan and South Korea combined in U.S.

apparel imports declined from 36.9 percent to 1.7 percent, replaced by the share of China's imports, which rose from 11.7 percent to 36.6 percent (see Chart 4.11). With new tariffs on apparel imports from China, the China's share will fall sharply, to be replaced by imports from Vietnam, Cambodia, Indonesia and Bangladesh. The total U.S. apparel imports may remain more or less the same. But this shift in the sourcing of imports away from China has already been occurring since 2010, because of the rise in labour costs in China and the appreciation of the Renminbi. This is similar to the earlier shift of the sources of U.S. imports of apparel from Hong Kong, South Korea and Taiwan to mainland China. The new U.S. tariffs will accelerate this process. The ASEAN and South Asian countries may benefit, but it is very hard to predict by how much because the supply chains today are so internationalised. However, it is unlikely, in most cases, that the tariffs will stimulate new employment-generating domestic production in the U.S.[24]

As expected, the trade war did not end before the U.S. mid-term elections on 6 November 2018. There is cautious hope that the temporary truce in the trade war, announced in the aftermath of the dinner meeting between President Trump and President Xi in Buenos Aires, Argentina on 1 December 2018, would eventually lead to a more lasting resolution. However, this is by no means certain. The real concern is that the trade war itself may do damage to the longer-term relation between China and the U.S. For example, it may affect the future rate of growth of U.S. exports of services to China[25], which consists mostly of education, tourism, and technology royalties and license fees, and in which the U.S. has a persistent, large and growing surplus, estimated to be US$55 billion by China and US$40 billion by the U.S. in 2017.[26] It may also affect the flow of direct as well as portfolio investment between the two countries.

---

24   While it may be possible to bring some production back to the U.S., it will be mostly through the use of automation and industrial robots, generating little actual new employment.

25   Exports of services from the U.S. have an almost 100 percent domestic value-added content.

26   See Xikang Chen, Lawrence J. Lau, Junjie Tang and Yanyan Xiong (2018).

Chart 4.11 The Distribution of U.S. Apparel Imports by Countries of Origin (1989–2017)

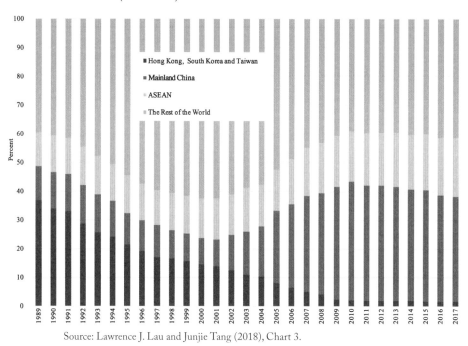

Source: Lawrence J. Lau and Junjie Tang (2018), Chart 3.

The Real Impacts on Selected Regions in China

Even though the real impacts on China's economy in the aggregate are relatively small, they can be more significant for specific individual municipalities, provinces and regions, especially those oriented towards exports. Guangdong, which includes Shenzhen, is the largest exporting province / municipality / autonomous region in China, accounting for more than 16 percent of China's total exports, followed by Shanghai and then Zhejiang. Guangdong's exports of goods to the world and to the U.S. were respectively 49.9 percent and 8.7 percent of its GDP in 2017 (see Chart 4.12), much higher than the respective national averages of 18.1 percent and 3.4 percent. Assuming the direct domestic value-added content of Guangdong exports to the U.S. is the same as that of China's exports as a whole, that is, 25 percent, the maximum loss in Guangdong's GDP in the first instance, assuming

Chart 4.12 Exports to the World and the U.S. as a Percent of GDP—Guangdong

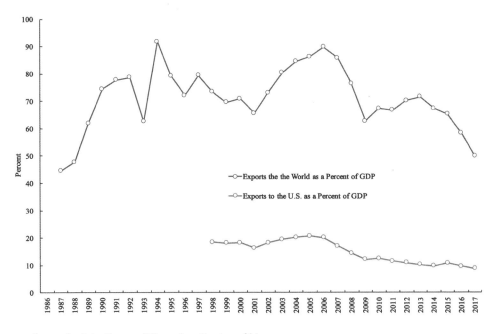

Source: Statistics Bureau of Guangdong Province, China.

that half of the exports to the U.S. are completely halted, may be estimated at 1.09 percent (8.7 / 2 × 0.25). Such a decline in GDP is manageable by Guangdong, as the real rate of growth of its GDP was 10.2 percent and its GDP per capita was US$12,909 in 2017. Taking into account the indirect, that is, second-, third-, fourth- and higher-round effects of the reduction of exports from Guangdong, the total domestic value-added affected increases to 66 percent. This implies ultimately a total loss in Guangdong's GDP of 2.87 percent (8.7 / 2 × 0.66). This will represent a significant slowdown in the real rate of growth of Guangdong's economy. Even then, it will still be growing at more than 7 percent per annum.

Exports as a percent of GDP in Zhejiang was just below 36.8 percent in 2017, and exports to the U.S. was 7.1 percent of its GDP (see Chart 4.13). Assuming the direct domestic value-added content of Zhejiang's exports to the U.S. is the same as that of China as a whole, that is, 25 percent, the maximum loss in Zhejiang's GDP, assuming that half of its exports to the U.S.

Chart 4.13 Exports to the World and the U.S. as a Percent of GDP—Zhejiang

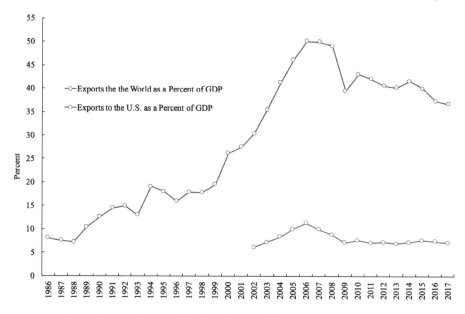

Source: Statistics Bureau of Zhejiang Province, China.

are completely halted, may be estimated in the first instance at 0.89 percent (7.1 / 2 × 0.25). A decline of this magnitude is manageable, as the real rate of growth of Zhejiang's GDP was 8.6 percent and its GDP per capita was US$14,630 in 2017. Taking into account the indirect, higher-round effects of the reduction of exports, the total loss in Zhejiang's GDP may be estimated to be 2.3 percent (7.1 / 2 × 0.66). This will also represent a significant slowdown in the real rate of growth of Zhejiang's economy, but the rate of growth would still be higher than 6 percent.

Within the province of Guangdong, Shenzhen Municipality has had the highest exports to GDP ratio. In 1990, Shenzhen exports amounted to almost 250 percent of its GDP (see the red line in Chart 4.14). Over the years, its export share has declined to 73.7 percent in 2017, with the share of exports to the U.S. at 11.3 percent, more than three times the national average of 3.4 percent and higher than the provincial average of 8.7 percent. If there is any devastating economic damage from the trade war, we should find it in Shenzhen. Assuming that the domestic value-added content of

Chart 4.14 Exports to the World and the U.S. as a Percent of GDP—Shenzhen

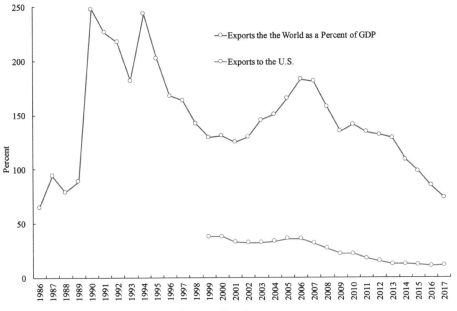

Source: Statistics Bureau of Shenzhen Municipality, China.

Shenzhen's exports to the U.S. is the same as that of China's exports to the U.S. as a whole, that is, 25 percent, the maximum loss in Shenzhen's GDP in the first instance, assuming that half of its exports to the U.S. are completely halted, may be estimated at 1.41 percent (11.3 / 2 × 0.25). Such a decline in GDP is manageable for Shenzhen, as the real rate of growth of its GDP was 8.8 percent and its GDP per capita was US$27,123 in 2017.[27]

Taking into account the indirect, that is, second-, third-, fourth- and higher-round effects of the reduction of exports from Shenzhen, the total loss of Shenzhen's real GDP may be estimated at 3.7 percent (11.3 / 2 × 0.66). This will represent a significant slowdown for Shenzhen's economy. Even then, the Shenzhen economy will still be growing at an annual rate of 5.1 percent, higher than the average rate of growth of the world economy of

27   See the Annual Economic Report of Shenzhen at http://www.sztj.gov.cn/xxgk/ zfxxgkml/tjsj/tjgb/201804/t20180416_11765330.htm.

3.7 percent, as forecast recently by the IMF for 2018 and 2019[28], and that of neighbouring Hong Kong, projected to be around 4.0 percent for 2018. The relatively high GDP per capita of Shenzhen will also help it to weather the trade war. However, if all China's exports to the U.S. were halted, it would imply a reduction in the rate of growth of Shenzhen of 7.4 percent (11.3 × 0.66), leaving Shenzhen with an anaemic but still positive annual rate of growth of 1.4 percent. The recently announced Guangdong–Hong Kong–Macau Greater Bay Area Initiative, which involves 11 cities in the Pearl River Delta region, amongst which are Hong Kong and Shenzhen, should provide some economic stimulus to mitigate the impacts of the trade war to the region.

Thus far, the trade war does not seem to have done too much noticeable damage to China's economy. In the third quarter of 2018, China's real GDP grew at a year-on-year rate of 6.5 percent, following the 6.7 percent in the second quarter. This was the lowest rate of growth of China's real GDP since the first quarter of 2009, when it grew 6.2 percent. Chart 4.15, in which the quarterly rates of growth of China's real GDP, year-on-year, are presented in colour-coded columns. It is clear from this chart that the rate of growth of China's real GDP has stabilised.[29]

At the regional level, the real GDP of Guangdong province grew by 6.9 percent during the first three quarters of 2018, better than the 6.7 percent for the same period in 2017. The real GDP of Zhejiang province grew by 7.5 percent in the first three quarters, a slight decline from the 7.6 percent in 2017. The real GDP of Shenzhen grew at 8.1 percent in the first three quarters, compared to 8.8 percent in 2017. Thus, the real impacts of the trade war were so far quite small, even for the export-oriented provinces and regions. It is perhaps still too early for the full effects of the trade war to show because the reduction of export orders received as a result of the trade

---

28   The IMF projection was published on 18 October 2018. The IMF also projected growth rates of 2.4 and 2.1 percent for the advanced economies for 2018 and 2019 respectively. The emerging and developing economies were projected to grow at 4.7 percent for both 2018 and 2019.

29   We should compare like-coloured columns so as to control for the seasonal effects.

Chart 4.15 Quarterly Rates of Growth of China's Real GDP (Year-on-Year)

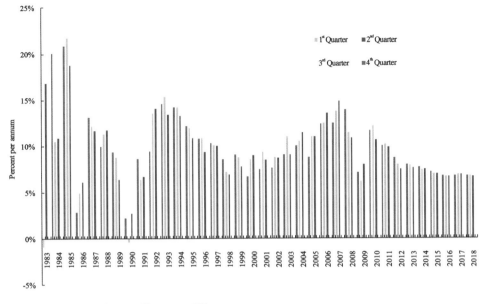

Source: National Bureau of Statistics of China.

war will not seriously affect production until late 2018 or early 2019. There is also the possibility that China's exporters accelerated production and delivery in order to beat the deadlines for the imposition of the new tariffs. However, as we have shown above, the negative impacts are manageable even under the worst scenario of total cessation of exports of goods subject to new U.S. tariffs.

The Real Impacts on the Economy of Hong Kong

What are the impacts of the trade war on the economy of the Hong Kong Special Administrative Region? Exports (and imports) have traditionally been extremely important for the Hong Kong economy. For the first century of Hong Kong's existence, it was a prosperous entrepôt connecting the economy of southern China with the rest of the world. Imports arrived from all over the world, including the mainland of China, to be re-exported to both the mainland and the rest of the world. There were very few Hong

Kong domestic exports, that is, exports of goods manufactured or produced in Hong Kong. All of this changed after the outbreak of the Korean War in 1950, when a trade embargo, led by the U.S. and the United Nations, was imposed on the mainland of China.

Hong Kong adjusted to the new situation by developing its light manufacturing industries, and gradually became a major exporter of garments, plastic flowers, toys, wigs and other light industrial goods. Domestic exports gained in importance as re-exports dried up because of the embargo. In 1973, total Hong Kong exports of goods was 63.1 percent of Hong Kong's GDP, out of which almost three quarters consisted of domestic exports (see Chart 4.16).

In Chart 4.16, the values of total exports of goods and services, exports of goods only, re-exports and domestic exports of Hong Kong since 1973 are presented.[30] Hong Kong's total exports of goods and services began to grow steadily as a percent of GDP beginning in the early 1980s, as entrepôt trade became possible once again with the economic reform and opening on the mainland. In the peak year of 2011, Hong Kong's total exports of goods and services to the world was a whopping 209.5 percent of Hong Kong's GDP, while total exports of goods only were 172.7 percent, implying exports of services of 36.8 percent of Hong Kong's GDP. The growth of exports of services was mostly due to the rapid growth of tourism, driven by the rising income on the mainland and the institution of the "individual visit scheme" of mainland tourists in 2005. By 2017, total exports as a percent of GDP had declined to 176.2 percent, with the exports of goods at 145.7 percent and the exports of services at 30.5 percent. Tourism remains a mainstay of the Hong Kong economy today. These figures show how dependent the Hong Kong economy was and still is on exports of both goods and services.

During this same period, the composition of Hong Kong's total exports has also changed dramatically. In 1984, domestic exports were 52.6 percent of Hong Kong's GDP. By 2017, it had fallen to only 1.6 percent! In the meantime, re-exports, almost all either destined for or originated

---

30   Unfortunately, published data on Hong Kong exports of services do not seem to be available prior to 1998.

Chart 4.16 Hong Kong's Total Exports of Goods and Services, Goods Only,
Re-Exports and Domestic Exports to the World as a Percent of
Hong Kong's GDP

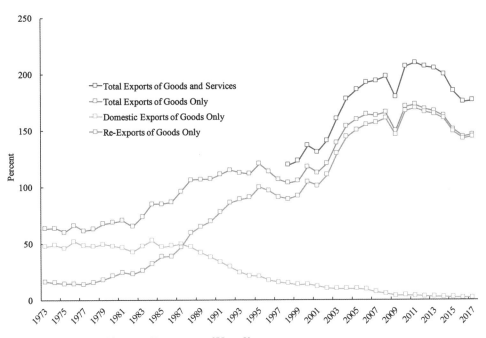

Source: Census and Statistics Department of Hong Kong.

from mainland China, grew from 15.8 percent of Hong Kong's GDP in
1973 to a peak of 169.3 percent in 2011. By 2017, it had fallen slightly to
144.1 percent, still a very large amount. The decline in the re-exports was
due to both the China's accession to the WTO and the development and
growth of ports in the mainland of China, which made it less necessary for
goods to pass through Hong Kong. However, it should be noted that the
domestic value-added content of re-exports is very low, not more than a
few percentage points, and mostly through the shipping terminals. Despite
re-exports constituting a large percentage of Hong Kong's GDP, its real
contribution to Hong Kong's GDP and employment does not compare
with that of tourism.

In Chart 4.17, the total exports of goods and services, exports of goods
only, re-exports, and domestic exports from Hong Kong to the U.S. are

presented. Hong Kong's domestic exports of goods to the U.S. are not subject to any of the new U.S. tariffs against China, whereas Hong Kong's re-exports of Chinese goods to the U.S. will be subject to the new U.S. tariffs and will be affected. Hong Kong's re-exports to the U.S. grow rapidly from 1.1 percent of Hong Kong's GDP to a peak of 23.3 percent in 2000, but by 2017 had fallen to 12.3 percent. However, as mentioned above, the domestic value-added content on Hong Kong's re-exports of Chinese goods to the U.S. is very low, so that the real impacts on the GDP of Hong Kong will be quite negligible. Hong Kong's domestic exports to the U.S. were a highly significant 23.4 percent of Hong Kong's GDP back in 1984, but by 2017 had fallen to an insignificant 0.1 percent. Hong Kong's exports of services to the U.S. amounted to 2.9 percent of Hong Kong's GDP in 2017. In any case, neither Hong Kong's domestic exports nor exports of services to the U.S. are subject to the new U.S. tariffs.

In conclusion, the direct real impacts of the China-U.S. trade war on the economy of Hong Kong will be quite small and certainly negligible. Whatever economic impacts there may be will be mostly indirect. For example, the Hong Kong stock market has already been negatively affected, such as the average price level[31], the volume of Initial Public Offerings (IPOs), the daily turnover, etc. Hong Kong direct investors on the mainland of China will be affected to the extent that the profits of their invested enterprises there are negatively impacted by the new U.S. tariffs. However, many of them have already diversified their operations to Vietnam, Cambodia, Bangladesh and Indonesia, and can substitute their exports to the U.S. with alternative sources not subject to the new U.S. tariffs.

Tourism from the mainland of China, an important mainstay of the Hong Kong economy, may also be affected to the extent that economic growth slows down significantly there. However, the prognosis is that the real impact on the mainland's economy is likely to be slightly more than 1 percent of GDP at a maximum. Tourism from the U.S. may also be affected by China-U.S. tensions. However, in the aggregate the impacts will be

---

31   See Chart 4.1 above.

Chart 4.17   Hong Kong's Total Exports of Goods and Services, Goods Only,
             Re-Exports and Domestic Exports to the U.S. as a Percent of
             Hong Kong's GDP

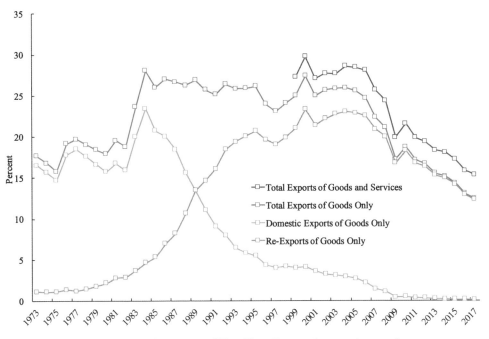

Sources: Census and Statistics Department of Hong Kong. Exports of services data are taken
from the Bureau of Economic Analysis, U.S. Department of Commerce.

relatively small. Before China's accession to the WTO and the expiration
of the Multi Fibre Arrangement, it was not unusual for goods produced
in China to be finished in Hong Kong and hence to be able to claim a
Hong Kong origin. However, this practice violates "country of origin" rules
in international trade and should not be allowed again, especially not during
the China-U.S. trade war.

The Real Impacts on the U.S. Economy

China has responded to the trade war by imposing new tariffs on a total
of US$110 billion of imports from the U.S., at a rate of 25 percent for the
first US$50 billion and 10 percent for the second US$60 billion. What are

the economic impacts of these tariffs on the U.S.? The dependence of the U.S., a large continental economy with a huge domestic market in terms of purchasing power, on exports is even lower than that of China. U.S. exports of goods and services combined as a share of its GDP was 12.1 percent in 2017 (see Chart 4.18). Its exports of goods alone as a share of its GDP was only 8 percent. The shares of U.S. exports of goods and services and goods alone to China in U.S. GDP was 0.97 percent and 0.67 percent respectively in 2017 (see Chart 4.19), much lower than China's exports to the world and to the U.S. as shares of China's GDP.

The direct domestic value-added content of U.S. exports of goods to China may be estimated to be 50.8 percent in 2015, about twice the value-added content of China's exports to the U.S. of 25 percent.[32] Thus, assuming that all of the exports of goods to China are completely halted, the maximum loss in U.S. GDP in the first instance may be estimated at 0.34 percent (0.67 × 0.508), less than the impact on China's GDP of 0.85 percent if all China's exports of goods to the U.S. are halted. Moreover, it is unlikely that all U.S. exports of goods to China will be halted; for example, computer chips will probably continue to be imported by China in large quantities. Suppose only half of U.S. exports of goods to China are halted, this would amount to a loss of U.S. GDP of 0.17 percent. This is not significant for the U.S. economy as a whole, especially with the recent recovery of the quarterly rate of growth of GDP to 4.2 percent in the second quarter of 2018.[33] U.S. GDP per capita was US$59,518 in 2017.[34] The U.S. economy can easily weather a reduction of 0.17 percent in its rate of growth.

With the indirect, that is, second-, third-, fourth- and higher-round effects of the reduction of U.S. exports of goods kicking in, the total domestic value-added (GDP) affected increases to 88.7 percent of the value of the reduced exports.[35] This implies ultimately a total loss in U.S. GDP of 0.30

---

32   See Xikang Chen and Wang Huijuan (2016), Tables 2.6 and 2.8.
33   See BEA News, https://www.bea.gov/news/2018/gross-domestic-product-2nd-quarter-2018-third-estimate-corporate-profits-2nd-quarter-2018.
34   This is calculated by dividing official U.S. GDP of 2017 by official U.S. mid-year population of 2017.
35   See Xikang Chen and Wang Huijuan (2016), Tables 2.6 and 2.8.

Chart 4.18 U.S. Exports of Goods and Services and Goods Only to the World as a Percent of U.S. GDP

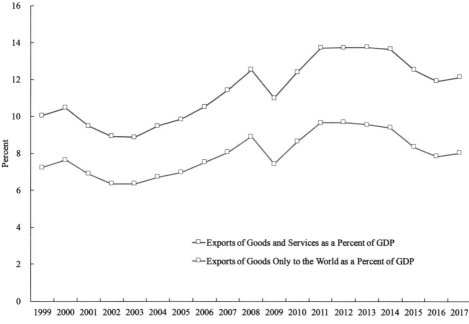

Sources: U.S. Census Bureau and U.S. Bureau of Economic Analysis.

percent (0.67 / 2 × 0.887), assuming that half of U.S. exports to China will be halted. In absolute terms, this amounts to US$58 billion (0.003 × 19.4 trillion) in 2017 prices, less than half of China's estimated loss in GDP of US$137 billion.

However, this is actually not a particularly opportune time for the U.S. to have a trade war with China. U.S. exports to China have been growing at a much higher rate than U.S. exports to the world (see Chart 4.20). This means that the huge and growing Chinese market can become a major growth point for U.S. exports if it is not interrupted by the trade war. In addition, the U.S. has a significant and growing trade surplus in services with China, estimated in 2017 to be US$40 billion by the U.S. government but US$55 billion by the Chinese government (see appendix Tables A3.3 and A3.4), which may be jeopardised if China-U.S. relations deteriorate further. A major share of U.S. exports of services to China is in the area of education

Chart 4.19 U.S. Exports of Goods and Services and Goods Only to China as a Percent of U.S. GDP

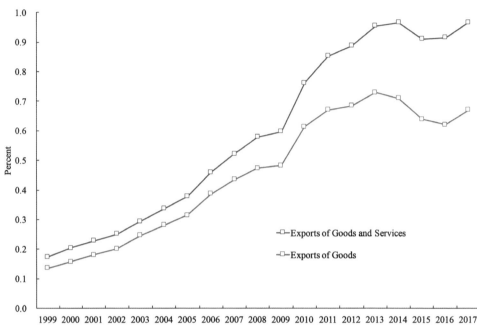

Sources: U.S. Census Bureau and U.S. Bureau of Economic Analysis.

and tourism. The expenditures of Chinese students (currently totalling 350,000) and tourists in the U.S. have been rising rapidly. Moreover, their presence in the U.S. can enhance understanding between the Chinese and American peoples and improve long-term ties. U.S. students and tourists in China can also play the same role.

Imposing tariffs on China's exports to the U.S. is unlikely to do the trick of eliminating the U.S.-China trade deficit because of the possibility of retaliation by China, which would reduce U.S. exports to China at the same time. The problem with a trade war is that there are no real winners—both countries lose because the feasible consumption choices open to each of them are artificially restricted and reduced. Exporters in both countries will be hurt because of the reduction in their exports, and importers in both countries will see their businesses decline. The consumers and producers

Chart 4.20 Annual Rates of Growth of U.S. Exports of Goods to the World and
          to China

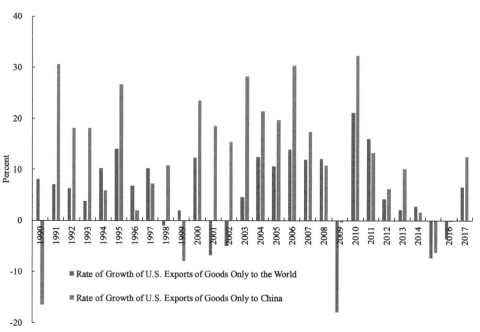

Sources: U.S. Census Bureau and U.S. Bureau of Economic Analysis.

who rely on imported goods and inputs in both countries will have to pay
higher prices. A serious trade war, however short in duration, is disruptive
in the sense that it introduces a great deal of uncertainty in future trade
and investment decisions. Moreover, if agreements can be easily overturned
and treaties can be readily broken, long-term trade agreements will have
little credibility or usefulness. The most likely net outcome of these new
country-specific tariffs is the substitution of imports from China by imports
from other countries on the part of U.S. importers and similarly by China's
importers. Thus, while the U.S. trade deficit with China falls, its trade deficits with other countries rise. The overall U.S. trade deficit with the world
will not be significantly altered, and neither GDP nor employment in the
U.S. will increase much.

President Trump's primary objective is to run and win re-election in
2020. He did promise to be tough on China to his supporters during his

presidential campaign in 2016. He used China as a villain and bash China in the mid-term elections as it was a popular theme with his base. Now that the U.S. mid-term elections are over, he might choose to ease up temporarily, or he might decide to become even more aggressive, looking forward to the presidential election in 2020. Given that the election outcomes were mixed and the potential opposition from the House of Representatives in which the Democrats now have a majority[36], it is difficult to predict what President Trump would do. Perhaps there would be a truce in the trade war. However, as we have analysed above, the economic losses from the trade war are manageable for both China and the U.S.

---

36   The expected Speaker of the House, Representative Nancy Pelosi, is also well known
      for her criticism of the Chinese government.

Appendix

Table A4.1   Weights Used in the CFETS Trade-Weighted Basket of Currencies

Currencies	Weights Used Before 2017	Weights Used Since 1 January 2017
USD (U.S. Dollar)	0.264	0.224
EUR (Euro)	0.2139	0.1634
JPY (Japanese Yen)	0.1468	0.1153
HKD (Hong Kong Dollar)	0.0655	0.0428
GBP (Pound Sterling)	0.0386	0.0316
AUD (Australian Dollar)	0.0627	0.044
NZD (New Zealnad Dollar)	0.0065	0.0044
SGD (Singapore Dollar)	0.0382	0.0321
CHF (Swiss Franc)	0.0151	0.0171
CAD (Canadian Dollar)	0.0253	0.0215
MYR (Malaysian Ringgit)	0.0467	0.0375
RUB (Russian Rouble)	0.0436	0.0263
THB (Thai Baht)	0.0333	0.0291
ZAR (South African Rand)	0	0.0178
KRW (Korean Won)	0	0.1077
AED (Arab Emirates Dirham)	0	0.0187
SAR (Saudi Riyal)	0	0.0199
HUF (Hungarian Forint)	0	0.0031
PLN (Polish Zloty)	0	0.0066
DKK (Danish Krone)	0	0.004
SEK (Swedish Krona)	0	0.0052
NOK (Norwegian Krone)	0	0.0027
TRY (Turkish Lira)	0	0.0083
MXN (Mexican Peso)	0	0.0169
Total	1.000	1.000

Source: CFETS.

Part II

Competitors and Partners: Challenges and Opportunities for China and the U.S.

5. Economic Complementarities

The economic complementarities of two economies are based on the size and other demographic characteristics of their populations, their relative natural endowments of land, water, mineral and other resources, their inherited stocks of tangible and intangible capital (including human capital and R&D capital), and the difference in their stage of development, which has important implications on the structure of their respective aggregate demands as well as supplies. But it is precisely these differences that create opportunities for the two economies to collaborate and to trade, and make them complementary. Two economies that are exactly the same in every way have nothing to sell to or buy from each other.

China and the U.S. are economically quite complementary. What is scarce in China is abundant in the U.S., and vice versa. For example, the U.S. is richly endowed with arable land and readily usable water on a per capita basis, but China is not. China has a huge supply of (surplus) labour, but the U.S. does not. American households are also very different: U.S. households are considered by the Chinese to be spendthrifts—they spend almost everything they earn and save very little; the Chinese households are typically disciplined savers. China and the U.S. are also at different stages of economic development. The U.S. economy has already entered a post-industrial phase, in which the service sector dominates; in China, the service sector has only just begun to pass the 50-percent mark in terms of its contribution to the aggregate GDP.

Comparison of Primary Inputs and Factor Proportions

In Table 5.1, we compare the primary inputs of China and U.S. economies with each other, such as labour (including population), arable land, tangible capital (including structures and equipment) and R&D capital. China's population is more than four times the U.S. population. The absolute quantities of arable land and tangible capital stock are not that different across the two economies. However, once they are put on a per capita or a per working-age population basis, the disparities become very clear. The U.S. R&D capital stock is almost four times as large as China's R&D capital stock.

Of course, it is not the absolute quantity of each of the primary inputs that matters. What matters is the quantity of the primary input relative to the population or the labour force. In Table 5.2, we compare the factor proportions of both economies. In terms of arable land per capita, the U.S. figure is almost five times the figure of China. Similarly, U.S. real tangible capital per capita is also almost five times the comparable figure of China. R&D capital per capita in the U.S. is 15 times higher than that in China. Thus, this would suggest that activities that are both capital- and R&D capital–intensive are much more favoured in the U.S. than in China.

Savings Rates and Capital-Labour Ratios

In Chart 5.1, we compare the savings rates of China, Japan and the U.S. We include Japan because it is the third largest economy in the world, and more importantly, to show that both China and the U.S. are, in a way, outliers. China has an exceptionally high savings rate, and the U.S. an exceptionally low one, by world standards. There are many reasons for savings rates to differ across economies: the stage of development; the level of real GDP per capita; the adequacy, maturity and reliability of the social safety net; the wealth-saving substitution, etc. This is not the place to examine why savings rates differ across countries, but to simply note that they are in fact very different. And despite a much higher investment rate in China, there is still excess savings in China that cannot be fully utilised productively within China. That is one of the causes of the massive excess manufacturing

Table 5.1   A Comparison of Primary Inputs—China and the U.S.

	China			U.S.		
	2015	2016	2017	2015	2016	2017
Population, thousand person	1,374,620	1,382,710	1,390,080	321,323	323,668	325,983
Arable land, thousand hectare	134,999	134,921	134,863	152,263	152,263	
Tangible capital stock, in 2016 prices, US$ billion	21,268	23,405	25,351	26,953	27,657	28,061
Real R&D capital stock, in 2016 prices, US$ billion	898	1,015	1,139	4,005	4,106	4,205
Working-age population (ages 15–64), person	996,030,376	995,072,896	993,792,919	212,357,568	213,254,816	213,911,387

Sources: Population—year-end for China from National Bureau of Statistics of China, and mid-year for the U.S. from U.S. Bureau of Economic Analysis. Arable land—for China from National Bureau of Statistics of China, and for the U.S. from the Food and Agriculture Organization of the United Nations. Tangible capital stock—estimated by Lawrence J. Lau from national income accounts data. Real R&D capital stock—estimated by Lawrence J. Lau and Yanyan Xiong (2018). Working-age population—from the World Bank's World Development Indicators (WDI) Database.

Table 5.2   A Comparison of Factor Proportions between China and the U.S.

	China			U.S.		
	2015	2016	2017	2015	2016	2017
Arable land per capita, hectare	0.098	0.098	0.097	0.474	0.470	
Real capital stock per capita, in 2016 prices, US$	15,472	16,927	18,237	83,880	85,448	86,080
Real R&D capital stock per capita, in 2016 prices, US$	654	734	819	12,463	12,685	12,900
Working age population per capita	0.725	0.720	0.715	0.661	0.659	0.656

Note: Figures for this table were calculated from Table 5.1 by the author.

production capacities found in China. It would therefore be beneficial for both China and the U.S. if the surplus Chinese savings could somehow be re-deployed in the U.S., where the domestic investment rate exceeds the domestic savings rate.

In the past, U.S. direct investment flows to China far exceeded China's direct investment flows to the U.S. American firms bring capital, technology, business methods and access to world markets to China. As Chinese enterprises grow and prosper, they also begin to expand and diversify, and begin to invest overseas. China's direct investment flows to the U.S. have been rising rapidly in recent years. However, the recently increased scrutiny

Chart 5.1   A Comparison of the Savings Rates of China, Japan and the U.S.

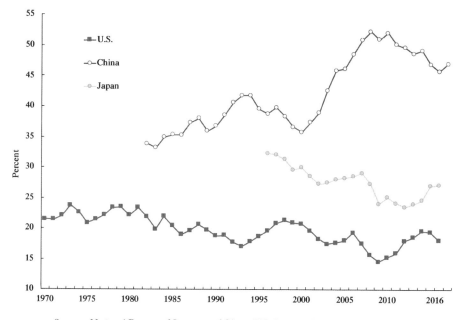

Sources: National Bureau of Statistics of China, U.S. Bureau of Economic Analysis, and the
World Bank's World Development Indicators (WDI) Database.

by the governmental Committee on Foreign Investment in the United
States (CFIUS) on direct investments from China may slow it down. Also,
as Chinese households become wealthy, they will want to diversity their
investment portfolios and begin to invest in capital markets in the U.S.
In time, as China's population ages, the elderly will begin to dissave, and
China's investments in the U.S. can then be repatriated to support China's
retirees in their silver years. We conclude that there is ample room for enhancing China-U.S. cooperation in the utilisation of the China's surplus
savings so as to achieve a more efficient use of savings and investments in
both countries.

But even with this high savings rate of China, the capital-labour
ratio in China has remained low in comparison with Japan and the U.S.

Chart 5.2   A Comparison of the Tangible Capital per Unit Labour in China, Japan and the U.S.

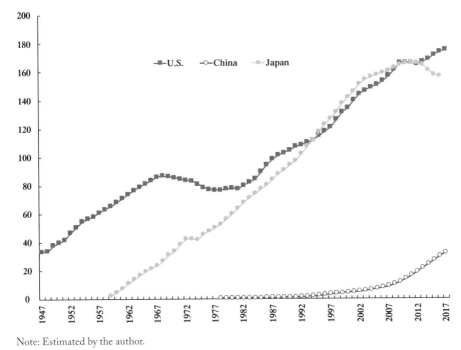

Note: Estimated by the author.

(see Chart 5.2).[1] The tangible capital per working age population of the U.S., at US$175,000 (in 2016 prices), is almost six times that of China's approximately US$32,000. This large difference in capital intensity is one major reason why an average U.S. worker is more productive than an average Chinese worker. It is also one reason why the Chinese economy still has a great deal of room for further rapid growth. It may seem like a paradox that an economy with such a high domestic savings rate as China still lags behind in terms of its capital-labour ratio. This basically has to do with the exceptionally large size of China's population and hence its labour force.

Another important determinant of the productivity of labour in an

---

1   It is not clear what caused the decline in the U.S. capital-labour ratio. It might be due to the "oil shock" in 1973, which caused much capital equipment to be written off.

economy is the quantity of human capital that has been accumulated over time. The proportion of China's working-age population with a Bachelor's degree or above is around 5 percent today. The comparable proportion in the U.S. is over 30 percent. This is a big gap, which can be closed only very slowly and gradually as a whole new generation of Chinese students goes to college.

A further kind of intangible capital is that of R&D capital. R&D capital is critical for innovation and technical progress. Tables 5.1 and 5.2 show that China on the whole is massively behind. This important topic will be specifically discussed in Chapter 7, in which China will be compared not only with the U.S. but also with selected countries and regions around the world.

The Tertiary (Service) Sector in the U.S. and Surplus Labour in China

Another dimension of economic complementarity is the difference between the distributions of GDP relative to employment by originating production sectors. China's distribution of GDP by originating production sectors in 2017 is 10 percent primary, 40 percent secondary and 50 percent tertiary (see Chart 5.3). By comparison, the U.S. distribution of GDP by originating production sectors in 2017 is 1 percent primary, 19 percent secondary and 80 percent tertiary (see Chart 5.4). China's distribution of employment by sector is 30 percent primary, 30 percent secondary and 40 percent tertiary (see Chart 5.5). The U.S. distribution of employment by sector is 1 percent primary, 15 percent secondary, and 84 percent tertiary (see Chart 5.6). China's service sector, which has been growing rapidly to become the largest sector over the past decade, can learn a great deal from the U.S. service sector in terms of technology, business models and operating procedures. Already this is the case—the fast food, online retail, and car-hailing services such as Uber, are ubiquitous in China. China's distribution of employment relative to GDP (30 percent versus 10 percent) in the primary sector also suggests that China still has a significant supply of surplus labour in the primary sector, whereas the U.S. has absolutely no surplus labour today (1 percent versus 1 percent). It also demonstrates the much higher efficiency

Chart 5.3 The Distribution of China's GDP by Originating Production Sector

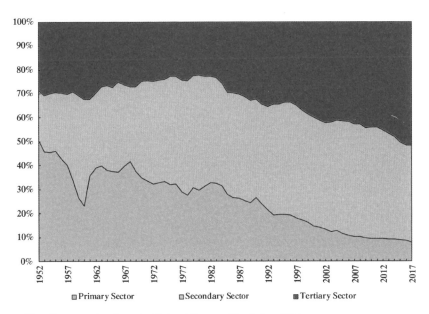

Note: Data are taken from the National Bureau of Statistics of China.

Chart 5.4 The Distribution of U.S. GDP by Originating Production Sector

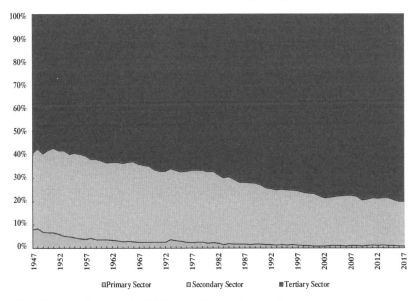

Note: Data are taken from the U.S. Bureau of Economic Analysis.

Chart 5.5   The Distribution of China's Employment by Production Sector

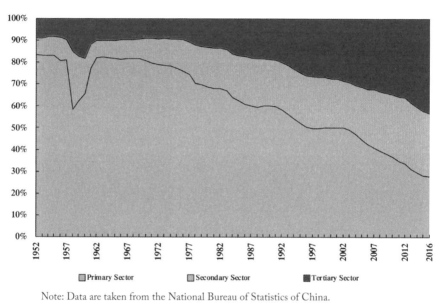

Note: Data are taken from the National Bureau of Statistics of China.

Chart 5.6   The Distribution of U.S. Employment by Production Sector

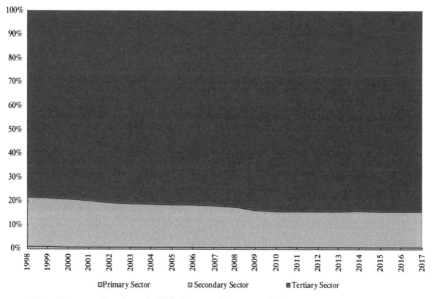

Note: Data are taken from the U.S. Bureau of Economic Analysis.

of labour in the U.S. primary sector.

The existence of significant surplus labour in the primary sector (70.5 percent) in 1978 justified the choice of light manufacturing by China as the focus of its export drive. From the viewpoint of the level of technology, China had to be content to leave the production of high value-added and high-tech products to developed economies such as the U.S. Initially, most of these foreign manufacturing investments were light manufacturing "processing and assembly"[2] operations aiming to use China as a production base for exports to the rest of the world[3], taking advantage of the low wage rates in China. In this way, China became the "world's factory". However, as China's real GDP per capita continued to grow while more and more Chinese households were able to join the middle class, China's real household consumption rose at a rate 1.5 times faster than its real GDP. China also became the "world's market".

Technology and Scale

The U.S. is a global leader in innovation and is far ahead of China in science and technological capabilities (see Chapter 7 for a more detailed discussion). China still relies on the U.S. for many of its needs, such as large aircraft and advanced semiconductors, to name only two. China will continue to need a great deal of technological support from the U.S. Of course, China has also been innovative in its own way: for example, the use of SMS in the initial stage of the mobile telephone and the use of WeChat Pay as a personal payment mechanism are both new, consumer-oriented Chinese innovations. But core internet technology and its communications software have basically been adopted by China from abroad.

---

2   "Processing and assembly" operations are manufacturing operations in which all intermediate inputs as well as equipment are imported and all output is exported. The only domestic input used is labour.

3   When China first opened to the world, the central plan remained mandatory. In order to avoid disruption of the fulfilment of the central plan, no outputs produced by foreign-invested enterprises could be sold in China, and no inputs other than labour could be bought in China.

The large size of China's market means that for many industries, economies of scale can be readily attained. The same is true of the U.S. economy. For high-tech products such as cell phones, whichever firm succeeds in winning customers in the two large markets will realise huge profits. With a single large market such as the U.S., it is already possible for a firm to amortise all of its development costs in a single market alone. With the addition of a second large market, the sales will be doubled, but the profits will be more than doubled because the fixed costs of development have already been fully amortised. The iPhone developed by Apple Inc. is such an example—it commands a large following in markets of both the U.S. and China. The high-tech consumer products area is where the market size pays off. Collaboration and cooperation among countries can be win-win for both producers and consumers. For example, the development of a common, or at least harmonised, 5G standard by both China and the U.S. should be good for all the high-tech firms in both countries.

In conclusion, we have identified many economic complementarities between China and the U.S. This means that there are many potential areas of mutually beneficial collaboration and cooperation. The trade war, which is lose-lose, should not be allowed to prevent the two countries from taking full advantage of all available opportunities.

6. Economic Competition

China's economic growth has been extraordinarily rapid since it began its economic reform and opening to the world in 1978. Growth accelerated after China's exchange rate reform in 1994, when China unified its multiple exchange rates, undertook a significant devaluation of the Renminbi, and implemented current-account convertibility. The rate of growth increased further after China's accession to the WTO in 2001 (see Chart 6.1). China's real GDP grew from US$369 billion in 1978 to US$12.7 trillion in 2017 (in 2017 prices). Since economic reform began in 1978, the Chinese economy has not had a single year of negative economic growth. Its average annual rate of growth over the past 40 years is just shy of 10 percent. The Chinese economy only began to slow down recently, after the global financial crisis of 2008.

Chart 6.1 shows the critical impact of China's economic reform and opening on its economy. There were large and unpredictable fluctuations in the rates of growth before the economic reform, resulting in very little improvement in the aggregate real GDP before 1978. Economic growth has been continuous, high and stable since the economic reform. Another useful observation is the importance of the size of the base level. Despite significantly higher rates of growth than the U.S. since 1978, China's aggregate real GDP was still significantly below U.S. real GDP in 2017. This is also true in the case of the real GDPs per capita of the two countries, which are compared in Chart 6.2.

The Chinese population has been growing continuously since 1978. Thus, the rate of growth of China's real GDP per capita has been lower than

Chart 6.1   Real GDP and Its Annual Rate of Growth—China and the U.S.

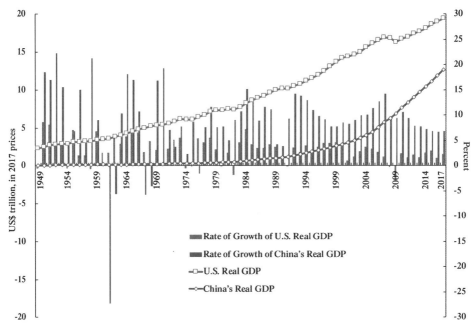

Sources: National Bureau of Statistics of China, U.S. Census Bureau and U.S. Bureau of Economic Analysis.

the rate of growth of China's real GDP. China's real GDP per capita grew from US$383 in 1978 to US$9,137 in 2017 (in 2017 prices) at an average annual rate of 8.1 percent, without any interruption, achieving an almost 23-fold increase (see Chart 6.2). China went from being a very poor country, with a GDP per capita barely above the subsistence level of one U.S. Dollar a day, to being almost a middle-income country[1], in just a little more than a generation. Even then, China as a country still only ranked below 70th in terms of real GDP per capita in the world. During the pre-reform period of 1949–1978, the average annual rate of growth of China's real GDP per capita was 5.2 percent.

---

1   The threshold for a middle-income country is often taken to be an annual GDP per capita of US$12,000.

Chart 6.2   Real GDP per Capita and Its Annual Rate of Growth—
China and the U.S.

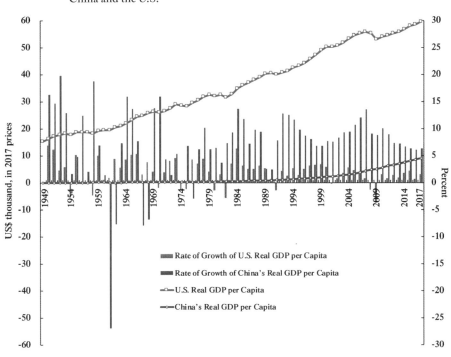

Sources: National Bureau of Statistics of China, U.S. Census Bureau and U.S. Bureau of
Economic Analysis.

Chart 6.2 compares the levels and rates of growth of the real GDPs per capita of China and the U.S. It shows that, in 2017 prices, despite China's much more rapid growth, China's real GDP per capita (US$9,137) still lags behind U.S. real GDP per capita (US$59,518), not quite one-sixth, and it is likely to remain behind for a long time.

In comparison with the U.S., China's real GDP went from only 20 percent of the U.S. real GDP in 2000 to two-thirds in 2017. It is only a matter of time before China's GDP will catch up with the U.S. GDP, probably in the early 2030s (see my projections in Chart 6.5 below). It is because of China's rapid economic growth that it is now viewed by the U.S. as a strategic competitor. The current China-U.S. trade war is only a reflection of the underlying China-U.S. competition for economic and technological dominance.

However, China's economic growth has not been, and is still not today, motivated by competition with the U.S. to be the largest economy in the world. It is motivated by the desire of the Chinese people to live better lives and to become moderately well-off. With a large population of 1.42 billion people, any significant improvement in the real GDP per capita will involve a significant increase in aggregate real GDP. We should always bear in mind that China's GDP per capita is only slightly more than US$9,000 (in 2017 prices) and not even one-sixth of the U.S. GDP per capita, even after 40 years of high rates of growth (see Chart 6.2). It is also worth noting that even though, by the last decade of the 19th century, the U.S. was already the largest economy in the world, it did not become the dominant power in the world until after the end of the World War II half a century later. In terms of real GDP per capita, China will likely lag behind the U.S. until the end of the 21st century.

Long-Term Projections of the Chinese and U.S. Economies

We present long-term projections of Chinese and U.S. real GDP up to 2050 in Chart 6.5 below. It is assumed that between 2018 and 2050, the Chinese economy will continue to grow at between 6 and 6.5 percent per annum for a few more years, then decline gradually to a rate between 5 and 6 percent, and that the U.S. economy will grow at an average annual rate of 3 percent.

Some may question whether the Chinese economy will be able to sustain such a high average annual rate of growth for such a long time. Experience around the world shows that the real rate of growth of an economy declines as its real GDP per capita rises. In Chart 6.3, the growth experiences of China, Japan and the U.S. are compared in the form of a scatter diagram between the rate of growth of real GDP and the real GDP per capita of the three countries. It shows that the rate of growth of real GDP does decline as the level of real GDP per capita rises. However, Chart 6.3 also shows that China today, with a still relatively low level of real GDP per capita (US$9,137) in 2017, operates within the range of a low level of real GDP per capita and so is still capable of a relatively high rate of growth

Chart 6.3   Real Rate of Growth versus Level of Real GDP per Capita—
China, Japan and the U.S.

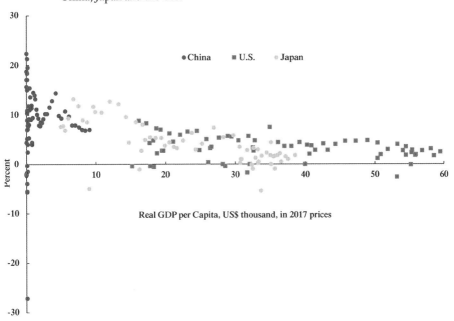

Source: Lawrence J. Lau, forthcoming (b).

for its real GDP. The average annual rate of growth of U.S. real GDP, when its real GDP per capita was between US$40,000 and US$50,000, was 3.7 percent.[2] However, the real GDP per capita of the Chinese economy is not projected to exceed US$40,000 in 2017 prices until 2045 (see Chart 6.6).

In addition, as we have shown in Chapter 5, the Chinese economy still has significant surplus labour in its primary sector. Chart 6.4 is a scatter diagram comparing the shares of employment in the primary sector versus the shares of GDP originating from the primary sector in selected countries and regions. The share of employment in China's primary sector was 27.7 percent, whereas the share of GDP originating from the primary sector was 8.6 percent. When Japan, South Korea and Taiwan had a comparable share

---

2   In the calculation of the average annual rate of growth, the recession year of 1991 has
     been left out.

Chart 6.4   The Share of the Primary Sector in Total Employment versus Its
            Share in GDP—Selected Economies

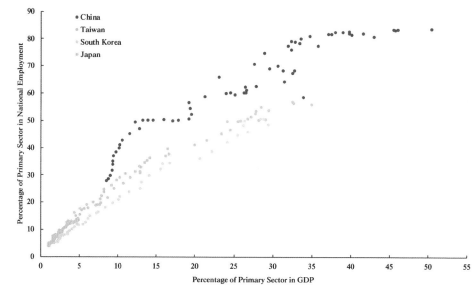

Source: Lawrence J. Lau, forthcoming (b).

of GDP originating from the primary sector, their shares of employment in
the primary sector were 24.7 percent, 17.9 percent and 21.5 percent respectively. This means that there still is significant surplus labour in China that
can be moved from the primary sector into the more productive secondary
and tertiary sectors, enabling China's real GDP to continue to grow at a
relatively high rate.

Moreover, as Chart 5.2 in Chapter 5 shows, China still had only a very
low level of tangible capital per unit labour[3] in 2017 (US$32,248 in 2016
prices) as compared to the U.S. (US$175,029), which means that there is
still quite a bit of room for the capital-labour ratio to increase and thereby
increase the productivity of labour. Furthermore, the Chinese economy has
yet to experience the stage of a high rate of technical progress or equivalent-

---

3   The denominator is measured as the sum of employment and unemployment, that is,
     the potential full employment.

Chart 6.5   Actual and Projected Levels and Rates of Growth of Chinese and U.S.
Real GDP (1978–2050)

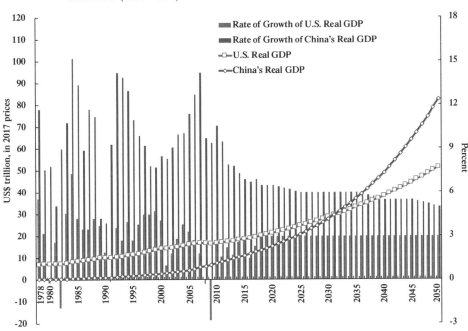

Sources: National Bureau of Statistics of China, U.S. Census Bureau, U.S. Bureau of
Economic Analysis and the author's estimates.

ly growth of total factor productivity. There also exist significant economies
of scale in the Chinese economy. Thus, a relatively high average annual rate
of growth of around 5 percent in China should still be possible for the next
several decades. Innovation, rather than tangible capital and labour, will
eventually become the principal driver of China's economic growth, just as
it is of the U.S. today, but it will take some time for this to happen.

The long-term projections of Chinese and U.S. real GDP are presented
in Chart 6.5, which shows that the aggregate China's real GDP will reach
the same level as the U.S. real GDP in 2031, at approximately US$29.4 tril-
lion in 2017 prices. By 2050, Chinese and U.S. real GDP are projected to be
US$82 trillion and US$51 trillion respectively. These projections are based
on what seem most likely at this time. It is possible for both the Chinese
and U.S. aggregate real GDPs to grow at rates different from what we have

Chart 6.6   Actual and Projected Chinese and U.S. Levels and Rates of Growth of
Real GDP per Capita (1978–2050)

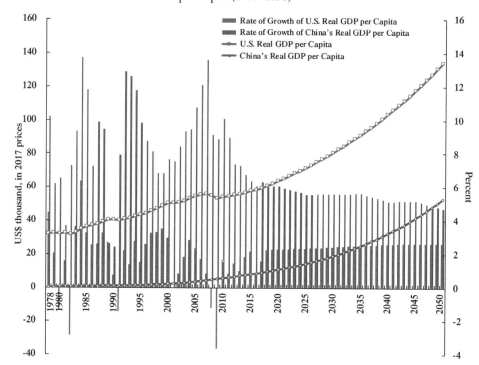

Sources: National Bureau of Statistics of China, U.S. Census Bureau, U.S. Bureau of
Economic Analysis and the author's estimates.

assumed here. However, I believe that it is unlikely for either China or the
U.S. to have a long-term average annual rate of growth that is significantly
higher than our assumptions.

   The long-term projections of Chinese and U.S. real GDP per capita are
presented in Chart 6.6, which shows that even with a significantly higher
growth rate, China's real GDP per capita will continue to lag behind the
U.S. real GDP per capita by a wide margin for decades to come. In 2050,
U.S. real GDP per capita is projected at US$134,000 (in 2017 prices), which
would be more than 2.5 times the projected China's real GDP per capita
of US$53,000 (in 2017 prices). My own projections suggest that it will be
at least the end of this century before the China's real GDP per capita can
catch up to the level of the U.S.

Table 6.1   A Comparison of the Ranks of China and the U.S. as Trading-Partner
Countries to the Top 20 Trading Nations in the World (2017)

Top 20 Trading Countries/Regions	Chinese Rank as Trading Partner of Country/Region	U.S. Rank as Trading Partner of Country/Region
Mainland China	NA	1
United States	1	NA
Germany	3	4
Japan	1	2
Netherlands	3	4
France	8	5
Hong Kong	1	2
United Kingdom	3	2
South Korea	1	2
Italy	5	3
Canada	2	1
Mexico	2	1
Belgium	7	5
India	1	2
Singapore	1	2
Spain	5	7
Russian	1	5
Switzerland	3	2
United Arab Emirates	1	4
Poland	7	10

Source: Compiled from IMF's Direction of Trade Statistics.

International Trade

China's share of world trade in goods and services has been growing rapidly
(see Chart 1.2 in Chapter 1). In Charts 3.2 and 3.3 in Chapter 3, we have
already seen that China is now the second largest trading nation in the
world, in goods and services combined, just after the U.S. It has, however,
also become the largest trading nation in goods alone. This is in part because
China is now not only the "world's factory", but also the "world's market".

In Table 6.1, we compare the ranks of China and the U.S. as trading-partner countries for the top 20 trading countries in the world in goods
only in 2017.[4] China and the U.S. were the largest and second largest trading

---

4   Data from IMF's Direction of Trade Statistics (available at http://data.imf.org/
     ?sk=9D6028D4-F14A-464C-A2F2-59B2CD424B85), including only trade in goods.
     Detailed bilateral data on trade in services are not available.

countries in goods respectively. In addition, China and the U.S. were the most important trading-partner countries of each other. Out of the top 20 trading countries in the world, China was the most important trading-partner country for eight of them, including the U.S., Japan, South Korea, India and Russia, while the U.S. was the most important trading-partner country for three of them (China, Canada and Mexico). China was a more important trading-partner country than the U.S. for 11 out of the 18 (excluding China and the U.S.) and the U.S. was a more important trading-partner country than China for 7 out of the 18. However, China now faces the challenge of transition as it begins to lose its comparative advantage in light manufactured goods but has yet to establish a competitive position in either heavy manufactured goods or in high-tech products such as advanced semiconductors. The U.S. remains the largest trading nation in services and runs a significant trade surplus in services with the rest of the world.[5]

The U.S. Dollar and the Chinese Yuan

China would like to see the Yuan (the Renminbi) used more widely in international transactions. At the present time, the Renminbi is used in the invoicing, clearing and settlement of only a little more than 15 percent of China's cross-border trade transactions (see Chart 6.7). Prior to 2010, almost all China's cross-border trade transactions were settled in U.S. Dollars; in 2010, China's cross-border trade transactions began to be settled in Renminbi. The Renminbi's share rose quickly and reached a peak of almost 35 percent in the third quarter of 2015. However, the sudden and unexpected devaluation of the Renminbi following the collapse of the Shanghai Stock Market that year caused a loss of confidence in the use of the Renminbi as an invoicing, clearing and settlement currency, especially by foreign exporters exporting to China. As a result, the share of Renminbi settlement fell to a little more than 15 percent and since then has managed to stabilise at that level.

---

5   We should bear in mind that the rankings apply to trade in goods only.

Chart 6.7   Renminbi Settlement of China's Cross-Border Trade

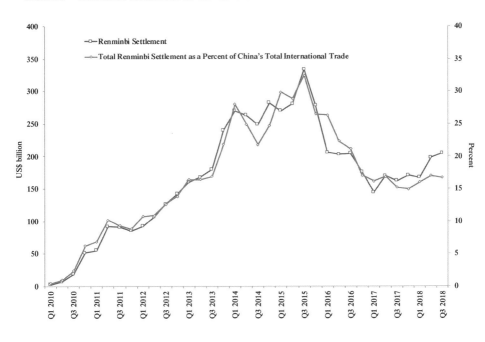

Source: National Bureau of Statistics of China.

Even then, because of the growth of China's international trade[6], by August 2018, the Renminbi had risen to become the fifth most widely used settlement currency after the U.S. Dollar, the Euro, the British Pound and the Japanese Yen, and accounting for 2.1 percent of world settlement. Chart 6.8 shows the shares of world settlement by the world's top 20 currencies, side by side with their respective shares of world trade. However, relative to the China's share of world trade of 9.75 percent, the Renminbi is significantly underutilised.[7] The U.S. Dollar, the most widely used settlement currency in the world, accounts for almost 40 percent of world settlement,

---

6   The inclusion of the Renminbi in the IMF's "Special Drawing Rights (SDR) Basket" might also have helped, as more central banks have become willing to hold some Renminbi as part of their official foreign exchange reserves.

7   This may be due, in part, to the lack of full convertibility of the Renminbi.

Chart 6.8   Comparison of the Share of World Trade (2017) with the Share of
World Settlement by Currency (August 2018)

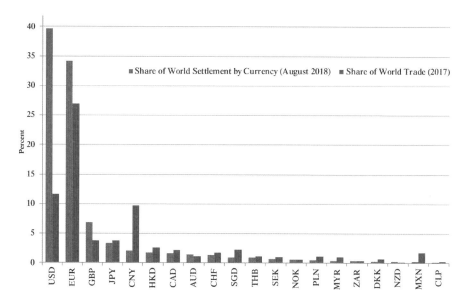

Sources: WTO database and Swift Renminbi Tracker.

even though the U.S. share of world trade in 2017 was only 11.7 percent.
This means that many third countries use the U.S. Dollar to settle their
transactions with one another, principally because they do not trust one
another's own currencies and do not wish to accept them. It is also precisely
for this reason that the majority of the central banks in the world hold
mostly U.S. Dollars in their official foreign exchange reserves, which are
readily accepted by other countries.

　　Thus, the U.S. performs a useful service by providing U.S. Dollars to be
used as an international medium of exchange (and a store of value) among
third countries. It can pay for its trade deficit with pieces of paper, such as
its currency and bonds, which it can print at will at almost zero marginal
cost. This can be a huge benefit. And this is what the U.S. has been able to
do since the early 1970s when it unilaterally abolished the convertibility to

gold, taking advantage of the seigniorage[8] derived from providing the only widely-accepted international medium of exchange.[9] In addition, the U.S. can exercise a great deal of leverage by controlling the access and use of the U.S. banking system by foreign nationals.

However, it is unlikely that the Renminbi will want to challenge the dominant position of the U.S. Dollar. In the short and medium term, the most feasible and likely goal of the Renminbi is to try to be more like the Japanese Yen. Japan settles almost 90 percent of its international trade transactions with its own currency (see Chart 6.8). If China can settle 90 percent of its cross-border transactions in Renminbi, it would amount to US$4 trillion per year in absolute value. It would certainly reduce the amount of official foreign exchange reserves that the People's Bank of China (China's central bank) needs to maintain. It is possible, over time, for the Renminbi to be a more widely used currency in Asia, including the ASEAN region and the Belt-and-Road countries.

Economic Self-Sufficiency

The degree of economic self-sufficiency or potential self-sufficiency in critical goods is also an important indicator of national economic strength. For example, military equipment and supplies can be critical goods. A country that cannot produce its own such goods is at the mercy of its supplier. Besides military goods, energy and food are also critical goods. No country can operate for long if there is insufficient energy or food. China is a large net importer of both energy and food. The U.S. has recently become a net exporter of energy, thanks to the advancement in shale oil and gas technology. It is also a large exporter of food and agricultural commodities. In contrast, China has supplanted the U.S. to become the largest oil importer in the world. It also increasingly relies on imports for its food supply, either directly or indirectly. This means that China is much more vulnerable to a

---

8   Seigniorage is also spelled "seignorage" or "seigneurage".
9   This benefit has been estimated to be worth as much as US$350 billion a year.

disruption in the supplies of energy and food. Its lack of self-sufficiency means that China is likely to be more vulnerable to external disturbances.

In summary, while the Chinese economy has made a great deal of progress in the past 40 years, and its aggregate real GDP is on the way to surpassing the aggregate U.S. real GDP in another decade and a half, its real GDP per capita will continue to lag behind the real GDP per capita of the U.S. for decades to come. China's international trade is also very competitive, but it faces the challenge of moving up in the value-chain as its wages rise and the exchange rate appreciates. The Renminbi cannot compete with the U.S. Dollar as an international medium of exchange or a store of value for a long time, and China is also nowhere near self-sufficient in critical goods. It will take a while for China to reach economic parity with the U.S.

7. Why is There a Technological Gap?[1]

One important indicator of the national economic strength of a country, in addition to real GDP and real GDP per capita, is its innovative capacity, which depends on its achieved level of science and technology. Even though China has made tremendous efforts and achieved significant progress in developing its science and technology, it still lags behind the U.S. generally, except in a few niche areas (such as high-speed trains and quantum communication). Sustained investment in research and development (R&D) and in human capital is essential for the occurrence of innovation in an economy. The development of human capital in China and the U.S. has been discussed in Chapter 5. In this chapter, we focus on the comparison of investment in R&D and the level of science and technology across countries and regions.

There are significant variations in the extent of investment in R&D across countries and regions. In Chart 7.1, the annual expenditure on R&D as a percent of GDP is presented for the Group of Seven (G-7) countries (Canada, France, Germany, Italy, Japan, the U.K. and the U.S.), the four East Asian Newly Industrialised Economies (EANIEs, including Hong Kong, South Korea, Singapore and Taiwan), China, and Israel.[2] The U.S. ratio, starting from a relatively low 1.32 percent in 1953, rose rapidly to 2.09 percent in 1957, partly as a reaction to the successful launch

---

1   A great deal of the information in this chapter has been taken from my joint research with Professor Yanyan Xiong of Zhejiang University. See Lawrence J. Lau and Yanyan Xiong (2018), Part I, Introduction.

2   Israel is included because it is a major R&D country.

Chart 7.1   R&D Expenditures as a Share of GDP—G-7 Countries,
             Four EANIEs, China and Israel

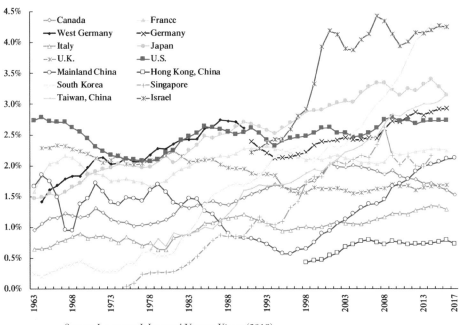

Source: Lawrence J. Lau and Yanyan Xiong (2018).

of the Sputnik I satellite by the former Soviet Union in the same year. It has since held steady between 2.07 percent and 2.79 percent over the last half a century, averaging 2.5 percent since 1963.

China's ratio started even lower, with less than 0.1 percent in 1953, but increased rapidly to a peak of 2.57 percent in 1960, comparable to the U.S. ratio of the same year. Between 1963 and 1984, China's ratio was actually higher than that of Canada[3], Italy and the four EANIEs. Then it plummeted below 1 percent, bottoming out in 1996 at 0.56 percent. Since then, it has been recovering steadily to reach 2.12 percent in 2017, once again surpassing the R&D expenditure to GDP ratios of Canada, Italy and the U.K., but still lagging significantly behind not only the developed economies of

---

3   With the exception of the Chinese Cultural Revolution years of 1966 and 1967.

Germany, Japan and the U.S., but also the newly-industrialised economies of South Korea and Taiwan. China's ratio was supposed to reach 2.2 percent in 2015, but failed to meet its goal. It is now targeted to reach 2.5 percent in 2020[4], the same as the long-term average ratio of the U.S. However, even at 2.5 percent of GDP, China's ratio will still be below the expected ratios of Germany, the U.S., Japan, South Korea, Taiwan and Israel.

West Germany's ratio was neck and neck with the U.S. ratio between 1975 and 1990.[5] However, after Germany's reunification in 1990, the unified Germany's ratio was below the U.S. ratio until 2010, when it finally managed to catch up. Japan's ratio was 1.47 percent in 1963 and rose steadily to overtake the U.S. ratio in 1989 and has remained significantly higher than the U.S. ever since. More recently, South Korea's ratio caught up with the U.S. ratio in 2004 and surpassed the Japan's in 2009. In 2016, Israel led the set of economies under study in Chart 7.1, with an R&D expenditure to GDP ratio of 4.25 percent, followed by South Korea at 4.23 percent. Hong Kong had the lowest ratio among the economies under study (0.73 percent in 2017).

The stock of real R&D capital, defined as the cumulative past real expenditures on R&D, less the depreciation of 10 percent per year, is a useful summary measure of the current potential capacity for innovation, as it typically takes years of cumulative effort before investment in R&D can pay off in terms of new discoveries and inventions. The initial real R&D capital stocks at the beginning of the years for which data on R&D expenditure are first available are not known and have been separately and individually estimated by Lawrence J. Lau and Yanyan Xiong (2018) for each economy. In Chart 7.2, our estimates of the real R&D capital stocks of selected econ-

---

4   *Guojia zhongchangqi kexue he jishu fazhan guihua gangyao* 國家中長期科學與技術發展
    規劃綱要 (2006–2020) (Outline of the national medium- and long-term scientific and
    technological development plan 2006–2020), available at http://www.most.gov.cn/kjgh/
    kjghzcq/.
5   From 1964 to 1990, R&D expenditure data are only available for West Germany. Thus,
    the R&D to GDP ratios (and the quantities of real R&D capital stock of West Ger-
    many) prior to 1991 are presented separately from those of the unified Germany, which
    are available since 1991.

Chart 7.2   Real R&D Capital Stocks—G-7 Countries, Four EANIEs,
               China and Israel

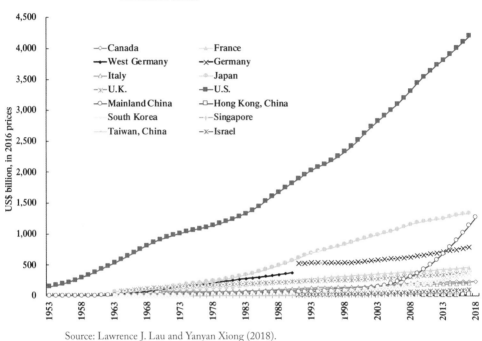

Source: Lawrence J. Lau and Yanyan Xiong (2018).

omies at the beginning of each year are presented. At US$4.21 trillion in
2017, the U.S. is clearly the world leader in real R&D capital stock, followed
by Japan, with US$1.34 trillion, as a distant number two. China's real R&D
capital stock has been growing rapidly since the early 2000s because both
its GDP and its R&D expenditure to GDP ratio have been increasing.
China has essentially caught up with most countries and regions in terms
of the level of real R&D capital stock, with the exceptions of the U.S. and
Japan (although China is poised to overtake Japan soon). However, even at
US$1.14 trillion in 2017, China's real R&D capital stock was still less than
30 percent of the corresponding U.S. R&D capital stock.

In Chart 7.3, the levels and the rates of growth of the real R&D capital
stocks of China and the U.S. are compared. It shows that even though the
rate of growth of China's real R&D capital stock has been significantly
higher than that of the U.S. (12.2 percent compared to 2.4 percent in 2017),

Chart 7.3 Real R&D Capital Stocks and Their Growth Rates—China and the U.S.

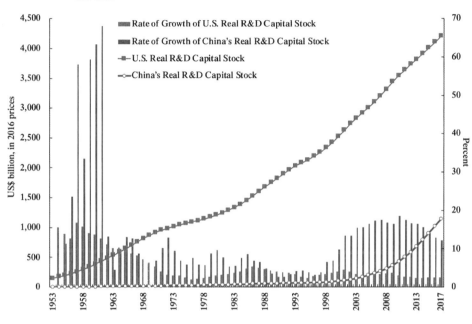

Note: Derived from Lawrence J. Lau and Yanyan Xiong (2018). The rate of growth of Chinese R&D capital stock in 1969 was −0.03 percent (not shown). It was the only year in which China's R&D capital stock had a negative rate of growth.

the level of China's real R&D capital stock still lags significantly behind that of the U.S. This will have a bearing on their relative rates of innovation, as the level of the real R&D capital stock of an economy is an important determinant of the annual number of patents that it is able to create.

Among R&D expenditures, three different categories—basic research, applied research and development—may be distinguished. Basic research is focused on the discovery of new knowledge, which we do not currently possess and may not have any immediate applicability or usefulness. Applied research is focused on answering a specific real-world question or solving a specific real-world problem. Development is focused on the creation of new products or services, or the improvement of existing products and services.

It is well known that "breakthrough" discoveries and inventions can occur consistently only in an economy with a strong foundation of basic

Chart 7.4   Basic Research Expenditure as a Share of Total R&D Expenditure—
Selected Countries and Regions

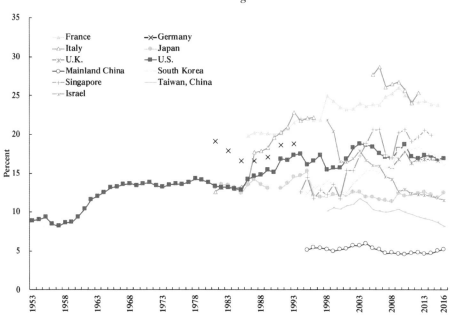

research. Thus, in the long run, leadership in innovation can only come about through significant investments in basic research. In Chart 7.4, the shares of R&D expenditure devoted to the support of basic research in each of the economies under study are presented.[6] Based on the available data, Italy and France led the group of economies under study with a basic research ratio of around 25 percent. The U.S. ratio averaged 17.3 percent during the ten years between 2007 and 2016. South Korea and the U.K. also had comparable ratios. Japan had a fairly stable ratio in the low teens. Taiwan's ratio was as high as 11.7 percent at its peak in 2003, but declined continuously since then, hitting 8.2 percent in 2016. China had the lowest ratio of basic research—between 5 and 6 percent.

As mentioned above, in order for breakthrough discoveries or inven-

---

6   Unfortunately, data on basic research expenditures are not available for some of the economies included in the study.

tions to be made, there must be significant investment in basic research over a sustained period of time. Basic research requires a long gestation period and has little or no immediate commercial or financial payoffs. It is therefore by definition patient and long-term research. Investment in basic research will imply a tradeoff of short-term gains for long-term rewards. The rate of return on investment in basic research, at any reasonable discount rate, will be low. It must therefore be financed by either the government or non-profit institutions, not by for-profit firms. The atomic and hydrogen bombs, nuclear reactors, the internet, packet transmission technology and internet browsers are all outcomes of basic research done many years before they were actually used in practical applications. However, China has the lowest share of basic research in total R&D expenditure among major economies, on average only around 5 percent, compared to 25 percent for France, 17 percent for the U.S. and 13 percent for Japan.

In Chart 7.5, a comparison of the real basic research capital stocks between China and the U.S. is presented. The real basic research capital stock is estimated as the cumulative real expenditure on basic research less an annual depreciation of 10 percent. China's real basic research expenditure prior to 1995, the first year for which data became available, is estimated on the assumption that China's ratio of basic research to total R&D expenditure was 5.13 percent, the same as the average annual ratio since 1995. The initial real basic research capital stock in 1953, the first year for which data were available, is assumed to be five times the real basic research expenditure in that year.[7] Chart 7.5 shows that the gap between the U.S. and China in the level of the basic research capital stock is even bigger than that of R&D capital stock in general. In 2017, China's basic research capital stock may be estimated to be US$56 billion in 2016 prices, less than 8 percent of the estimated U.S. basic research capital stock of US$723 billion. This difference may explain to some extent the differences in the numbers of Nobel Laureates in the fields of physics, chemistry and physiology or medicine between the two countries, which will be discussed below.

One useful indicator of the degree of success in innovation is the

---

7   It turns out that the estimates of the real basic research capital stock are not sensitive to plausible alternative assumptions on the initial real basic research capital stock in 1953.

Chart 7.5   The Level and Rate of Growth of Real Basic Research Capital
            Stock—China and the U.S.

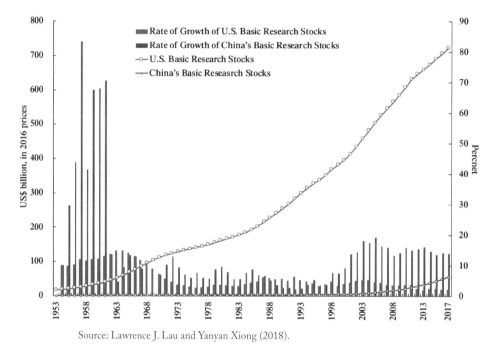

Source: Lawrence J. Lau and Yanyan Xiong (2018).

number of patents created (received) each year.[8] In Chart 7.6, the annual
number of patents granted domestically to domestic applicants[9] by the
relevant domestic patent authority for each of the economies under study
is presented. The big surprise of Chart 7.6 is the meteoric rise of China,
from 38 domestic patents granted in 1985 to 302,136 patents granted in
2016, the highest number in the world that year. China overtook Japan,
the long-time champion, in 2015. The U.S. and South Korea were in the
third and fourth places respectively. France, Germany and the U.K., which
used to rank right after Japan and the U.S., had all fallen behind in terms

8   The patents considered in this study are exclusively "invention patents". Data on patents
     is collected from the World Intellectual Property Organisation (WIPO), the United
     States Patent and Trademark Office, and the State Intellectual Property Office of the
     People's Republic of China.
9   A domestic applicant is a resident in the economy at the time of the application.

Chart 7.6   The Number of Domestic Patents Granted to Domestic Applicants—
G-7 Countries, Four EANIEs, China and Israel

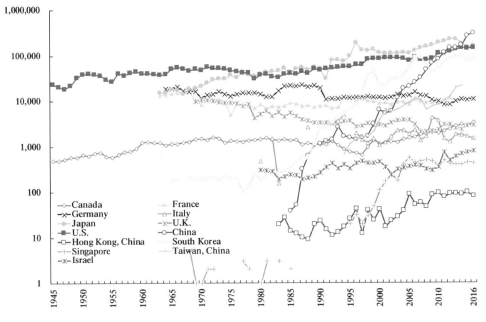

Source: Lawrence J. Lau and Yanyan Xiong (2018), Part I, Introduction.

of the number of domestic patents granted. Hong Kong was in last place among our set of economies, with 78 domestic patents granted to domestic applicants. However, Hong Kong was actually granted 601 patents by the U.S. Patent and Trademark Office (USPTO) in 2015, which would suggest that the small number of domestic patents granted to domestic applicants in Hong Kong was due to the lower domestic patent application rate caused by the relative unimportance of the Hong Kong market to its domestic discoverers and inventors.

The extraordinarily rapid rise in the number of China's domestic patent grants signifies China's determination to become an innovative country. Moreover, with such a large number of domestic patents granted in China each year, it can be expected that there will be widespread demand for the strengthening of the enforcement of intellectual property rights in China by the Chinese discoverers and inventors themselves.

Chart 7.7   Three-Year Moving-Average Domestic Patent Application Success
Rates—G-7 Countries (excluding Italy), Four EANIEs (excluding
Hong Kong), China and Israel

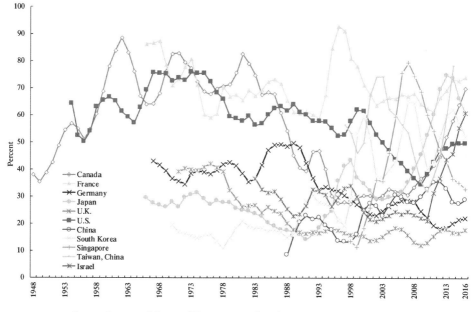

Source: Lawrence J. Lau and Yanyan Xiong (2018), Part I, Introduction.

Of course, it is not unreasonable to question the standards applied in the
approval of these domestic patent applications. In Chart 7.7, the three year
moving-average of the success rates of domestic applications (defined as the
number of domestic patents granted to domestic applicants divided by the
number of domestic applications submitted by domestic applicants, lagged
by one year[10]) are compared across our set of economies.[11] These rates vary
significantly across economies and also fluctuate over time. In 2016, France
had the highest domestic patent application success rate (74.1 percent)

---

10   One could also have chosen a two-year lag for the number of domestic applications. It
     all depends on the time required for processing of patent applications by the relevant
     domestic patent authorities. However, we believe that by using a three-year moving-av-
     erage of the success rates, we can avoid most of these timing problems.

11   The economies that have a higher number of U.S. patent applications than their num-
     ber of domestic patent applications are not included in Chart 7.7, as domestic appli-
     cants are obviously not interested in obtaining domestic patents, mostly because of the
     small size of the domestic markets.

Chart 7.8   U.S. Patents Granted—G-7 Countries, Four EANIEs, China
and Israel

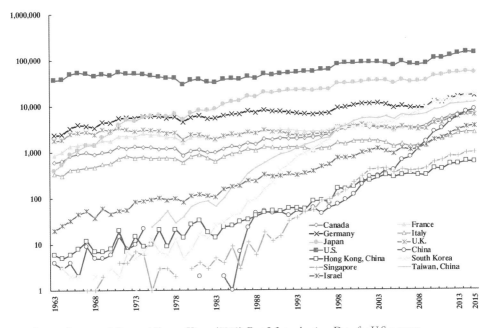

Source: Lawrence J. Lau and Yanyan Xiong (2018), Part I, Introduction. Data for U.S. patents granted are not available separately for West Germany. Thus, only data for a unified Germany are included.

among the economies under study, followed by Japan (60.9 percent), South Korea (52.2 percent) and the U.S. (49.8 percent). China's domestic patent application success rate was only 29.0 percent, much lower than those of France, Japan, South Korea and the U.S. This is at least prima facie evidence that China's patent authorities have reasonably stringent standards. Only Germany and the U.K. had lower domestic patent application success rates.

The annual numbers of patents granted by the USPTO to the residents of the different countries and regions, including the U.S. itself, are presented in Chart 7.8. This chart provides a useful comparison of one indicator of the relative success of R&D efforts across different countries and regions. Since these are patents granted in the U.S. by the USPTO, the U.S. may have a "home court" advantage. However, for all the other countries and regions, the comparison across them should be reasonably fair. Chart 7.8 shows that

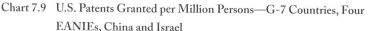

Chart 7.9   U.S. Patents Granted per Million Persons—G-7 Countries, Four
            EANIEs, China and Israel

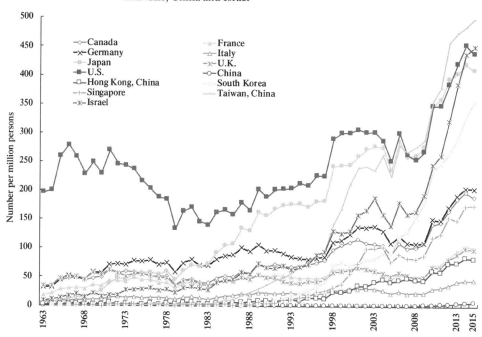

Source: Lawrence J. Lau and Yanyan Xiong (2018), Part I, Introduction.

the U.S. is the undisputed champion over the past 50 years with more than 140,969 patents granted in 2015, followed by Japan with 52,409 patents, and then by South Korea (17,924) and Germany (16,549). The number of U.S. patents granted to Chinese applicants each year increased rapidly from single-digit levels before the mid-1980s to 8,166 patents in 2015. The number of U.S. patents granted to applicants from Taiwan was 11,690 in 2015, ahead of China, Canada, France, the U.K. and Italy. In contrast, the number of U.S. patents granted to Hong Kong residents was only 601 in 2015.

In Chart 7.9, the number of patents granted in the U.S. by the USPTO each year to applicants from different countries and regions, including the U.S. itself, divided by the population of the respective countries and regions, is presented. On a per capita basis, the U.S. was the world champion until 2007 when it was overtaken by Taiwan and Japan. In 2015, the latest year for which published data on U.S. patents is available, Taiwan was the leader with 498 U.S. patents granted per million persons, followed by Israel (450), the U.S. (439), Japan (410), South Korea (354) and Germany (204). China, because of its large population, was in the last place among the economies under study, with slightly less than six U.S. patents granted per million persons in 2015. However, this may also be due, in part, to China's low application rate for U.S. patents (defined as the number of U.S. patent applications divided by the number of domestic applications submitted by domestic applicants in the same year) of only 2.2 percent. China's low application rate for U.S. patents may be due in part to the lack of English language facility on the part of Chinese discoverers and investors, to the cost of U.S. patent filing, and possibly to the fact that the Chinese domestic market is already quite large. South Korea had the next lowest U.S. patent application rate in 2015 of 22.8 percent[12] among the economies under study.

The three-year moving-average success rates of patent applications filed in the U.S. each year by the residents of different countries and regions, including the U.S. itself, over time, are presented in Chart 7.10. In recent years, Japan has had the highest success rate at 60.8 percent, and China had the lowest success rate at 46.0 percent, with the U.S. at an intermediate 49.8 percent.[13] The success rates of almost all countries and regions, including the U.S. itself, showed strongly synchronous fluctuations over time, with the possible exception of some outliers in the early years, indicating possible systemic changes in the procedures or standards used in the approval process of the USPTO in specific years. However, the fluctuations appeared to apply fairly uniformly to applicants from all the countries and regions, including domestic U.S. applicants, indicating that there was no obvious bias either in favour of or against applications from specific countries or regions, including the U.S. itself. (Italy's success rates were quite erratic, especially in the early years, because of large fluctuations in the number of its patent applications from year to year.)

---

12   See Lawrence J. Lau and Yanyan Xiong (2018).

13   This may be taken as evidence that there is no obvious "home court" bias in the U.S. patent grants.

Chart 7.10 Three-Year Moving-Average U.S. Patent Application Success Rates—
G-7 Countries, Four EANIEs, China and Israel

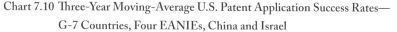

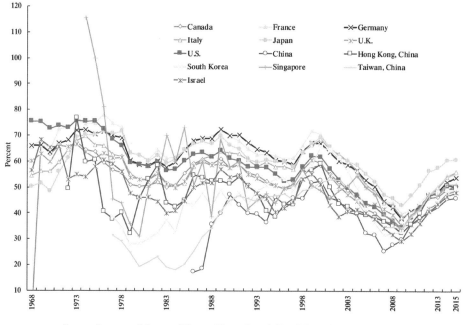

Source: Lawrence J. Lau and Yanyan Xiong (2018), Part I, Introduction.

The level of the real R&D capital stock of an economy can be shown
to have a direct causal relationship to the number of patents granted to the
residents of that economy. In Chart 7.11, the annual number of domestic
patents granted to the residents of a country or region is plotted against the
level of its real R&D capital stock at the beginning of that year.[14] It shows
clearly that the higher the level of the real R&D capital stock of an economy, the higher the number of domestic patents granted to its residents.
The estimated linear regression line in Chart 7.11 indicates a statistically
highly-significant positive relationship between the natural logarithm of
the number of domestic patents and the natural logarithm of the quantity
of real R&D capital stock. Roughly speaking, a one-percent increase in the

---

14   Data for real R&D capital stocks for a unified Germany are available only after 1991.
      Also note that the axes of Chart 7.11 are scaled logarithmically.

Chart 7.11 Domestic Patents Granted and Real R&D Capital Stock—
G-7 Countries, Four EANIEs, China and Israel

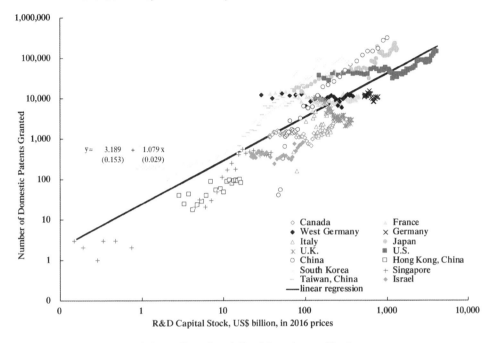

Source: Lawrence J. Lau and Yanyan Xiong (2018), Part I, Introduction. Numbers in parentheses are estimated standard errors.

real R&D capital stock leads to a 1.08-percent increase in the number of domestic patents granted. Moreover, the estimated elasticity of patents with respect to the quantity of real R&D capital, 1.08, is statistically significantly different from unity, indicating the existence of significant economies of scale in the creation of domestic patents.

However, it is worth noting that on an individual country or region basis, the positive correlation is not so obvious for the European G-7 countries (see for example France, West Germany, Italy and the U.K.) and for the early phase of the U.S. It is further worth noting that Japan and two of the EANIEs, South Korea and Taiwan, may be regarded as "over-achievers", in the sense that at any given level of real R&D capital stock, they were able to achieve higher numbers of domestic patents granted than the numbers predicted by the linear regression line. In contrast, Hong Kong and Singapore may be regarded as "under-achievers", in the sense that at any given level of real R&D capital stock, they were only able to achieve lower numbers of domestic patents granted than those predicted by the linear regression line, although this may well be due in part to the fact that they themselves have very small domestic markets and hence their discoverers and inventors may not find it worthwhile to apply for domestic patents. Finally, China was an "under-achiever" prior to 2000 but transformed into an "over-achiever" after 2000. In 2016, the number of domestic patents granted in China was more than six times what would have been granted if China had stayed on the linear regression line.

A word of caution is necessary in the interpretation of the domestic patents data above, as the different economies may well have their own different standards in the granting of domestic patents; moreover, these standards may also have changed systematically over time. What is unmistakable is the overall positive relationship between the number of patents granted and the level of the real R&D capital stock.

In Chart 7.12[15], the annual number of U.S. patents granted to the residents of a country or region is plotted against its real R&D capital stock at the beginning of that year. It also shows clearly that the higher the level of the real R&D capital stock of a country or region, the higher the number of U.S. patents granted to its residents. The estimated linear regression line is also statistically highly significant. Roughly speaking, a one-percent increase in the real R&D capital stock leads to a 1.15-percent increase in the number of U.S. patents granted. Moreover, on an individual economy basis, the positive correlation is apparent even for the G-7 countries.[16] We may further note that the estimated elasticity of patents with respect to the quantity of real R&D capital, 1.15, is statistically significantly different from

---

15   Data for real R&D capital stocks are not available for a unified Germany before 1990. Data for U.S. patents granted are not available separately for West Germany. Thus, only data for a unified Germany are included in Chart 7.12. Also note that the chart's axes are scaled logarithmically.

16   This is consistent with the view that the standards used by the USPTO are more stable than those of the patent authorities of the individual economies. This also confirms that the U.S. patent grants data are more comparable across economies.

Chart 7.12 U.S. Patents Granted and Real R&D Capital Stock—G-7 Countries, Four EANIEs, China and Israel

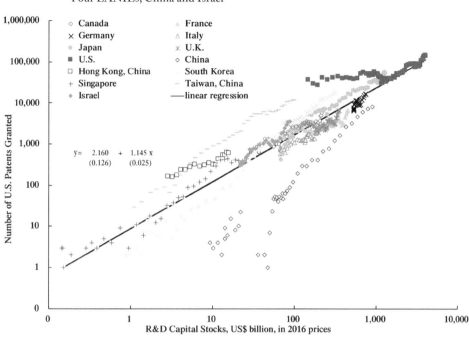

Source: Lawrence J. Lau and Yanyan Xiong (2018), Part I, Introduction. Numbers in parentheses are estimated standard errors.

unity, again indicating the existence of significant economies of scale in the creation of U.S. patents.

In terms of the creation of U.S. patents, the EANIEs, including even Hong Kong, have all turned out to be "over-achievers" (South Korea and Singapore since 1991). However, China stands out as a significant "under-achiever" in the sense that it was only able to achieve a much lower number of U.S. patents granted than that predicted by the estimated linear regression line.

The positive relationship between the number of patents granted and the level of the real R&D capital stock is stronger for U.S. patents granted (Chart 7.12) than for domestic patents granted (Chart 7.11). This may be due to the more uniform standards on patent grants on the part of the USPTO as opposed to the different domestic patent-granting authorities, and also possibly to self-selection on the part of the non-U.S. applicants who might choose to submit applications only for patents perceived to be of higher quality and therefore more likely to be granted. Taken as a whole, the overall positive relationship between the number of patents granted, whether domestic or U.S., and the level of the real R&D capital stock, are clearly and unmistakably established. The higher the level of the real R&D capital stock, the higher is the number of patent grants. Thus, investment in R&D is a critical driver of innovation. Moreover, there also appears to be significant economies of scale in the creation of patents, so it should not be a surprise that the economies with the highest levels of R&D capital stocks produce proportionally even greater numbers of patents.

The "over-achievement" and "under-achievement" identified above may actually reflect significant systematic differences in not only the efficiency in the creation of domestic and U.S. patent grants across economies, but also in the standards used by the patent-granting authorities of the different economies. Thus, China appears to have higher-than-average efficiency in the creation of domestic patents but lower-than-average efficiency in the creation of U.S. patents.[17] We believe that the relative efficiencies in the creation of U.S. patent grants are probably more reliable because all economies face the same uniform standards of the USPTO, as opposed to the possibly differing standards maintained by the respective individual domestic patent-granting authorities.

In addition to patent grants, another important indicator of scientific and technological achievements is the number of science and engineering articles published in professional journals, as well as the frequency of their citations. In Chart 7.13, the annual number of science and engineering articles published by the residents of selected countries and regions is presented. It shows that in 2016, China overtook the U.S. in terms of the total number of articles published (426,165 to 408,985); this is after the U.S. had had a huge lead over all other economies for many years. In Chart 7.14, the

---

17   The low Chinese efficiency in the generation of U.S. patents may have been caused, in part, by the exchange rate used in the conversion of China's real capital stocks from 2016 Renminbi into 2016 U.S. dollars.

Chart 7.13 The Number of Science and Engineering Articles of Selected
            Economies

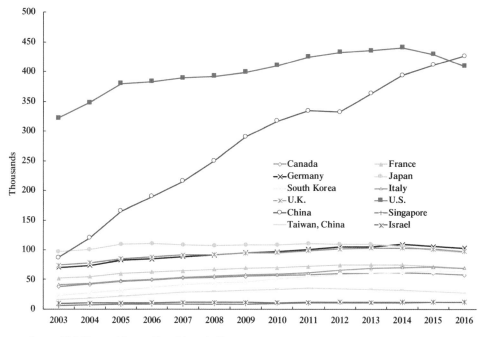

Source: U.S. National Science Board (2018), Chapter 5.

share of each country or region in the world total of published science and
engineering articles is presented. It shows that China accounted for 18.6
percent and the U.S. accounted for 17.8 percent of the total in 2016.

However, even though China was able to catch up with the U.S. in
terms of the total absolute number of science and engineering articles published, the quality of China's articles is still not quite comparable to that of
the U.S. articles. The number of times a published article is cited by another
author from abroad may be taken as an indicator of the quality and influence
of the article and its author (it is considered more reliable than a citation
from a person of the same country). The shares of citations to science and
engineering articles of China and the U.S. received from authors abroad between 1996 and 2014 are presented in Chart 7.15. This chart indicates that
the share of citations received by China's articles from authors abroad has

Chart 7.14 Science and Engineering Articles of Selected Economies as a Percent of the World Total

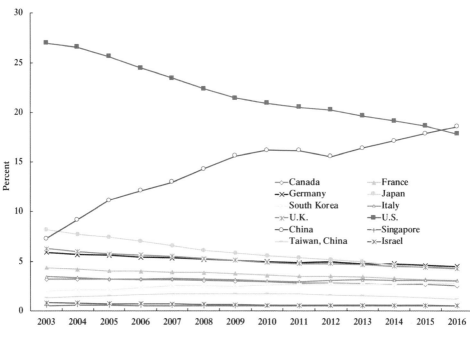

Source: U.S. National Science Board (2018), Chapter 5.

been declining and that the corresponding U.S. share has been rising and overtook China's share in 2001.[18] This may be due, in part, to the explosive growth of the total number of science and engineering articles published by Chinese authors (see Chart 7.13). There may simply be too many of them to receive the attention of authors abroad. But it may also be due, in part, to the possible deficiency in the comprehensibility of English articles written by Chinese authors. However, this latter problem should disappear over time as the language capability of Chinese scholars improves.

---

18   It is worth noting that both Japan and India had a higher share of citations received from authors abroad than the U.S. and China since 1998.

Chart 7.15 The Share of Citations to Science and Engineering Articles in China
           and the U.S. Received from Authors Abroad (1996–2014)

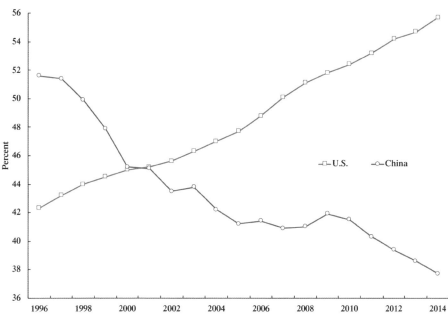

Source: U.S. National Science Board (2018), Chapter 5, Figure 5.27.

The Quality of Tertiary Educational Institutions

Another useful indicator of the national capacity for innovation is the quality of tertiary educational institutions. In Chart 7.16, the number of tertiary
educational institutions of Canada, China, France, Germany, Italy, Japan,
the U.K. and the U.S. that rank in the top 100 in the world, according to
the Shanghai Jiaotong University rankings, are compared over time. There
are of course many other possible university rankings. We use the Shanghai
Jiaotong rankings because they are completely formulaic and do not depend
on any purely subjective assessments. They are hence more objective and
also completely replicable. The Shanghai Jiaotong rankings also put a high
weight on research achievements. Chart 7.16 shows that the U.S. has an

Chart 7.16 The Number of Tertiary Educational Institutions in the Top 100 in the World

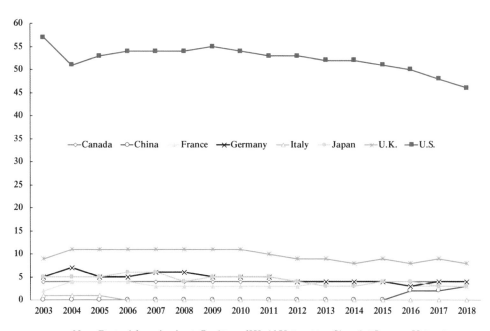

Note: Derived from Academic Ranking of World Universities, Shanghai Jiaotong University (2003–2008) and Shanghai Ranking Consultancy (2009–2018), various years.

overwhelming lead within the top 100 universities in the world with 46 institutions in 2018, followed by the U.K. with eight institutions. In 2018, Australia had six, Switzerland had five and the Netherlands had four (not included in this chart). China did not have any university in the top 100 in the world until 2016. It tied with France, Japan and Sweden in the eighth place in 2018, with three universities included each. If we restrict consideration to only the top ten universities in the world, the U.S. has had eight of them since 2003 and the U.K. the remaining two.

It is interesting to note that all of the best three countries in the list of top 100 universities (the U.S. with 46, the U.K. with eight, and Australia with six) have English as their official language and the principal language of instruction in their tertiary educational institutions. Most major international scholarly journals are also published in English. This may have introduced some bias against those countries and universities that use different languages. However, even if this bias can be corrected, it is unlikely to alter the conclusion that the U.S. has overwhelmingly the best universities in the world.

Can a Chinese university achieve the top ranks of world universities? It will probably take at least a couple of decades before the best of the Chinese universities can catch up to the same level as the best U.S. universities, and even longer for the Chinese share of the top universities to approach the U.S. share. However, it is not impossible. During the 20th century, three U.S. universities, Massachusetts Institute of Technology (MIT), Stanford University and the University of Southern California (USC), rose to become top-ranked universities in the world. MIT did it during the inter-war years, Stanford did it in the 1960s and USC did it in the 1980s. The necessary ingredients are talent (both faculty members and students), resources and fully committed leadership. There is no shortage of talent in China, with its large population—there must be an abundance of talent in the upper end of the population distribution. The best graduates of Chinese universities go overseas to the best universities to pursue advanced graduate studies and will return eventually to become faculty members in the best Chinese universities. There is also no shortage of resources in China today for investment in higher education and R&D. And there is full commitment on the part of the Chinese government. In time, some Chinese universities will be among the best in the world.

The Cumulative Number of Nobel Prizes Received

Still another useful indicator of relative national scientific strength at the level of the breakthrough frontier is the cumulative number of Nobel Prizes that the nationals of a country have received in the fields of physics, chemistry, and physiology or medicine since the Nobel Prizes were started in 1901. For the purpose of this analysis, the nationality of a Nobel Laureate is determined by the citizenship of the Laureate at the time of the announcement of the award. A shared award is counted fractionally. For example, if the prize in a given year is split 50 percent to an American citizen, 25 percent

Chart 7.17 The Cumulative Number of Nobel Prizes in Physics Received by
         Nationals of Canada, China, France, Germany, Italy, Japan, the U.K.
         and the U.S.

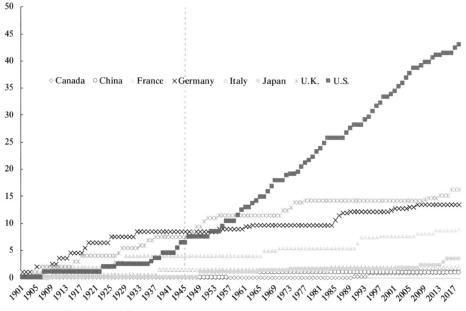

Note: Derived from the Nobel Prize website.

to a British citizen and 25 percent to a German citizen, it will count as ½, ¼
and ¼ respectively for the three countries. A laureate with dual nationality
will have the number or fraction divided equally between the two countries.

   112 Nobel Prizes in Physics were awarded to 210 laureates between
1901 and 2018. In Chart 7.17, the cumulative numbers of Nobel Prizes
in Physics received by nationals of Canada, China, France, Germany, Italy,
Japan, the U.K. and the U.S. are presented. In this field, Germany had the
highest cumulative number of Nobel Laureates until 1947, when it was
overtaken by the U.K. The U.S. did not become the leader of the world in
terms of the cumulative number of Nobel Laureates until 1960 but has had
a commanding lead since then (43.1 in 2018). France (9.1), Germany (13.6)
and the U.K. (16.3) combined have a cumulative total (39) that is actually
not that far behind the U.S. China had one Nobel Prize (shared between

Chart 7.18 The Cumulative Number of Nobel Prizes in Chemistry Received by Nationals of Canada, France, Germany, Italy, Japan, the U.K. and the U.S.

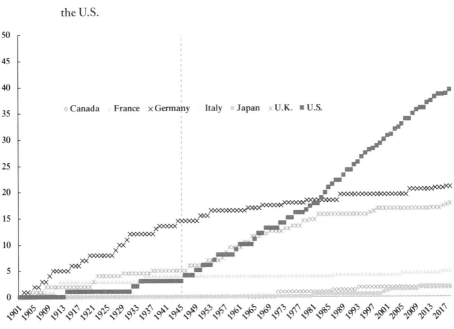

Note: Derived from the Nobel Prize website.

T. D. Lee and C. N. Yang[19]) in 1957 and that was the only one as of 2018.

110 Nobel Prizes in Chemistry were awarded to 181 laureates between 1901 and 2018. In Chart 7.18, the cumulative numbers of Nobel Prizes in Chemistry received by the nationals of the G-7 countries—Canada, France, Germany, Italy, Japan, the U.K. and the U.S.—are presented. In this field, Germany had the highest cumulative number of Nobel Laureates until 1981, when it was overtaken by the U.S. The U.S. caught up with France in 1946, became more or less even with the U.K. between 1951 and 1967, surpassed Germany in 1981, and by 2018 had accumulated a fairly commanding lead (39.4). However, if the cumulative numbers of Nobel Laureates of France

---

19   Both Professors T. D. Lee and C. N. Yang were Chinese citizens at the time of the announcement of their awards.

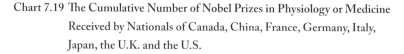

Chart 7.19 The Cumulative Number of Nobel Prizes in Physiology or Medicine Received by Nationals of Canada, China, France, Germany, Italy, Japan, the U.K. and the U.S.

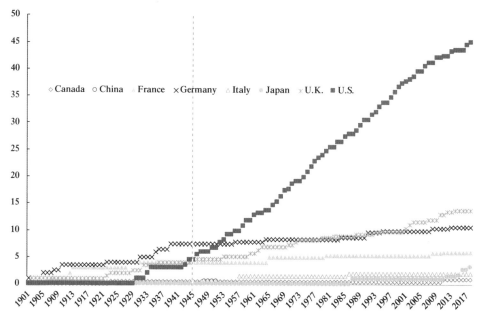

Note: Derived from the Nobel Prize Website.

(5.0), Germany (21.0) and the U.K. (17.9) are combined, the total (43.9) is actually higher than that of the U.S. Western Europe still has a strong foundation for research in chemistry. However, to date, no Chinese citizen has ever been awarded a Nobel Prize in Chemistry.

109 Nobel Prizes in Physiology or Medicine were awarded to 216 laureates between 1901 and 2018. In Chart 7.19, the cumulative numbers of Nobel Prizes in Physiology or Medicine received by nationals of Canada, China, France, Germany, Italy, Japan, the U.K. and the U.S. are presented. In this field, Germany had the highest cumulative number of Nobel Laureates until 1952, when the U.S. surpassed it to become the leader of the world in terms of the cumulative number of Nobel Laureates and has maintained a commanding lead ever since (45.1 in 2018). Even if the number of laureates of France (6), Germany (10.7) and the U.K. (13.8) are combined, the cumulative total (30.5) is still quite far behind that of the U.S. A Chinese citizen,

Tu Youyou, shared a Nobel Prize in Physiology or Medicine in 2015.[20]

It is clear that the U.S. has the largest cumulative number of Nobel Laureates in all three of the scientific prize categories to date. However, it was only in the post–World War II period, after 1945, that the U.S. made the most progress. The transition of scientific leadership from Western European countries such as France, Germany and the U.K. to the U.S. was facilitated by the migration of European scientific and engineering talent to the U.S. before, during and after World War II. Even then, it took a while. The U.S. had its first physics laureate in 1907 but did not surpass Germany in the cumulative total number of physics laureates until 1955. For the chemistry prize, the time gap between the first U.S. chemistry laureate in 1914 and the U.S. assuming leadership in terms of the cumulative number of chemistry laureates in 1983 was almost 70 years. For the physiology or medicine prize, the time gap was 22 years.

China is currently way behind the U.S. in terms of the overall development of science and technology at the frontiers, as reflected in the very small cumulative total number of Chinese Nobel Laureates (1.5 by our criterion of nationality).[21] It will likely take at least one generation, perhaps even two, before China can catch up to the level of scientific leadership of the U.S.

A Nobel Prize in one of the scientific fields normally requires a breakthrough discovery or invention. A breakthrough discovery or invention is frequently the outcome of long and patient years of basic research. The relative neglect of basic research in China may be one reason for its low cumulative number of Nobel Laureates. In addition, a cultural factor may have also held back the Chinese. The Chinese, or more generally East Asians, have a strong tradition of respect for authority and seniority, which makes it less likely for them to challenge established orthodoxies, an attitude that is necessary for a breakthrough discovery or invention. If Albert Einstein had not questioned the well-established Newtonian Laws, he would have

---

20   Tu Youyou shared the 2015 Nobel Prize in Physiology or Medicine with William C. Campbell and Satoshi Ōmura.

21   There have been other ethnically Chinese laureates that were not Chinese nationals at the time of the announcement of their awards, such as Professor Charles K. Kao (2009 Physics Prize) and Professor Yuan T. Lee (1986 Chemistry Prize).

never discovered the theory of special relativity, not to mention the theory of general relativity.

Other problems of China's scientific and technological development include the very short-term focus and the frequent duplication of R&D efforts. The short-term focus and emphasis on quick returns biases R&D efforts against basic research and in favour of applied research and development. The effects are already apparent in Charts 7.4 and 7.5. The duplication of R&D efforts not only wastes valuable resources but may also significantly delay the achievement of the R&D objective if the critical resources are spread too thin. An example is the development of an advanced semiconductor manufacturing capability in China, which is a worthy objective in itself. However, the critical bottleneck in China is not funding but the scarcity of qualified engineers and scientists. If there are too many such parallel projects going on simultaneously, none of them will have sufficient qualified manpower to make it a success. It will also amount to a huge waste of resources, as the establishment of a new pilot manufacturing facility typically requires a minimum investment of a couple of billion U.S. dollars.

Technological competition between China and the U.S. can potentially lead to constructive and positive, as well as destructive and negative, outcomes. For example, the competition on building the fastest super-computer in the world has already resulted in both countries producing better and faster super-computers. The champion in 2018 was the IBM Summit, a U.S. super-computer that beat the Sunway TaihuLight, the champion in 2016 and 2017, a Chinese super-computer built entirely with indigenously designed and produced chips. This is not unlike the launch of the Sputnik I satellite by the Soviet Union back in 1957, which spurred the development of science and technology in the U.S. in competition with the Soviet Union. The U.S. subsequently won the race to send a man, Neil Armstrong, to the moon in 1969.

The recent ZTE case illustrates how dependent some Chinese high-tech firms are on U.S. suppliers. ZTE, a major mobile telephone manufacturer in China, relies on chips designed by Qualcomm and manufactured by Intel. So, when the U.S. Department of Commerce prohibited U.S. firms from selling to ZTE as part of a punishment for circumventing the sanctions against Iran, it was like a death sentence for the firm. Even though the prohibition has since been lifted, the imports of the semiconductors may be subject to Chinese tariffs resulting from the China-U.S. trade war. By comparison, Huawei, another major Chinese mobile telephone and server manufacturer, designs its own chips through the wholly-owned subsidiary HiSilicon, which ranks as the seventh largest chip design company in the world.[22] It is therefore relatively unaffected by the trade war. In time, China will have to develop its own advanced semiconductor manufacturing capability, including the production of semiconductor manufacturing equipment. It will take some time though.

An arms race is also a form of competition. In terms of the total number of nuclear-armed warheads, the U.S. is way ahead of China by at least an order of magnitude, and even more in per capita terms. This is not a competition that China should wish to join. However, a race to find an effective cure for cancer or Alzheimer's disease would be worthwhile for both countries and in fact for the entire world. China-U.S. cooperation in the development of a common fifth-generation (5G) mobile communications standard would benefit consumers not only in China and the U.S., but also anywhere else in the world. If a common standard is not possible, then at a minimum the standards should be harmonised so that the same cell phone, regardless of the origin of manufacture, can be used everywhere in the world. Other areas of potential beneficial scientific and technological cooperation between China and the U.S. include the mitigation of climate change, R&D on nuclear fusion and space exploration.

Governments have an essential role to play in the support of R&D, especially basic research and research with military applications. The Chinese and U.S. governments are no exception. The U.S. government has financed research through the Defence Advanced Research Projects Agency (DARPA[23]), the Department of Energy, the National Institutes of Health,

---

22　James Kynge (2018), p. 11. The designed chips are then manufactured by the Taiwan Semiconductor Manufacturing Corporation in Taiwan.

23　DARPA, formerly known as the Advanced Research Projects Agency (ARPA), was established in 1958 as an agency of the United States Department of Defence and is responsible for the development of emerging technologies for use by the U.S. military.

and the National Science Foundation. It helped organise and provided an initial funding of US$500 million to Sematech, a partnership between the U.S. government and a consortium of 14 U.S.-based semiconductor manufacturers to improve semiconductor manufacturing in the U.S. Similarly, the Chinese government has also supported R&D through agencies such as its Department of Science and Technology and its National Natural Science Foundation. It has also funded the establishment of pilot manufacturing facilities for advanced semiconductors and nuclear reactors.

In conclusion, in spite of much progress, China still lags behind the U.S. significantly in the overall level of science and technology. It will probably take at least a generation for China to catch up to the same overall level of scientific and technological capability as the U.S., although it is possible for China to achieve parity with or even exceed the U.S. level in some special and relatively narrow niche areas (quantum communication, for example). Despite the competition from China, the U.S. is not likely to lose its leadership position in science and technology anytime soon.

However, even though Chinese scientists have so far not made many breakthrough discoveries and inventions, they have been very innovative and boldly experimental with practical, mass consumer-oriented applications, especially in the use of mobile communications and the internet to serve the needs of China's consumers. Some years ago, the Chinese were pioneers in eMessaging (SMSs) before the world caught on. They have since leapfrogged in eBanking and ePayment and even in eLending. China's individual consumers used to be underserved in banking services because there were and still are no personal checking accounts in China. However, cashless and paperless payment applications such as WeChat have transformed the situation completely. It is now possible for individuals to transfer funds to each other in real time from cell phone to cell phone with no hassle by simply scanning the QR codes. The scale of eRetailing in China is probably much greater than that in the U.S. today. All these innovations have been accomplished by entrepreneurs in the private sector.

8. Enhancing Mutual Economic Interdependence

To reduce the probability of an armed conflict between China and the U.S. down the road, it is necessary to build mutual trust between the two countries. Mutual trust can be gradually built through continuing long-term mutually beneficial economic interactions. If both countries can promote greater mutual economic interdependence to make their economic relations win-win, a war between them would be unthinkable, just as another war between France and Germany—which fought three wars between them (1870, 1914 and 1939) in less than 80 years—is not possible today.

The problem with a trade war as an instrument for reducing a bilateral trade deficit is that, while it may reduce the bilateral trade surplus or deficit, there are no real winners—both countries lose because the feasible choices open to each of them are reduced. Exporters in both countries will be hurt because of the reduction in their exports, and importers in both countries will see their businesses decline. The consumers and producers who rely on imported goods and inputs in both countries will have to pay higher prices. A better way to narrow the U.S. trade deficit with China is for the U.S. to increase its exports of goods and services to China, especially newly created goods and services—for example, by producing and exporting meat (beef, pork and poultry) instead of feed grains (corn and soybeans) to China, and selling the newly-developed liquefied natural gas from Alaska and shale oil from the continental U.S. to Chinese customers now that the U.S. has become a net energy exporter. However, it is important that the trade in these essential commodities such as food and energy be on a long-term basis, at pre-determined price formulae and with credible enforcement provisions against interruptions. Only then will new long-term supplies and demands emerge, and only then will there be long-term mutual economic interdependence.

In Chapter 3, we have shown that the overall U.S.-China trade deficit, appropriately measured, was only US$111 billion in domestic total value-added terms, as compared to the U.S. official estimate of US$376 billion for goods only. This means that if China can import an additional US$111 billion of U.S. goods in total value-added terms, there will be no U.S.-China trade deficit. The focus should therefore be on importing additional U.S. goods with a high domestic value-added content. This will not only enable the trade gap in terms of value-added to be closed more quickly, but will also ensure that the benefits of the additional U.S. exports to the U.S. itself in terms of GDP is maximised.

China and the U.S. should exploit their mutual economic complementarities, as discussed in Chapter 5. The two economies are very different. They are at very different stages of their development: China is still a developing economy in terms of its real GDP per capita, and the U.S. has been a mature, developed economy for more than a century. The Chinese people are still in the process of increasing their consumption and accumulation of physical things, such as appliances and automobiles, but the U.S. people are already over the stage of "physical things" and mostly focus on consuming services and leisure. The two economies also have very different comparative advantages: China has a very large population but relatively little arable land and other natural resources. The U.S. has far fewer people and much more arable land and other natural resources, including an abundant supply of various forms of energy. However, it is precisely these large differences between the two economies that enable them to derive potentially large gains from their economic exchanges with each other. Two economies that are similar to each other are likely to excel in producing similar goods and services, and hence are more competitive with—rather than complementary to—each other. As we have seen from Chapter 5, there are many complementarities between the Chinese and U.S. economies.

The China-U.S. trade war is clearly lose-lose for both countries. However, there is a much better alternative to the trade war. The U.S. trade deficit with China can be reduced by the U.S. increasing its exports of goods to

China instead of by China's decreasing its exports to (and imports from) the U.S. Moreover, there are two different ways for the U.S. to increase its exports of goods. The first way is by re-directing its existing exports of goods to other countries to China; the second way is by producing new outputs specifically for exporting to China, by employing domestic resources that are currently underutilised. The first way is actually mostly cosmetic. U.S. GDP and employment would not increase much, even though the U.S.-China trade deficit would fall. There is little real net benefit to the U.S. (or, for that matter, to China[1]), except to be able to claim that the U.S.-China trade deficit has been successfully reduced. The second way, however, would lead to genuine increases in GDP and employment in the U.S., and augment the supply of goods needed in China. U.S. producers, workers and exporters would benefit, as would Chinese consumers and producers who use the new imported goods, and Chinese importers. Both countries would be better off.

More fundamentally, almost all mainstream economists, American and otherwise, agree that the aggregate U.S. trade deficit with the rest of the world as a whole cannot be reduced without a corresponding reduction in the U.S. investment-savings imbalance. In other words, unless investment is decreased or savings is increased in the U.S. itself, the U.S. trade deficit with the rest of the world will remain essentially the same, whatever happens to the U.S.-China trade deficit. Selective country-specific protectionist policies, such as import tariffs and quotas, can succeed in shifting the source of the trade deficit—for example, from a U.S.-China trade deficit to a U.S.-ASEAN trade deficit—but cannot reduce the aggregate total U.S. trade deficit with the rest of the world. This is indeed true if the level of the U.S. real GDP is taken as given. We should recall that long before the Chinese economy opened to the world, the large U.S. trade deficit was at one time with Japan, and then successively with Hong Kong, Taiwan and South Korea.[2]

---

1   This is because the total world supply for the good is not increased. If China wishes to buy more than what it has been buying from other countries, it will raise the world price of the good to all buyers, including China itself.

2   That was when "voluntary export restraints" and the Multi Fibre Arrangement (1974–2004) were introduced.

However, there is an important exception—if an *autonomous* (unanticipated) increase in the demand for exports from the U.S. increases the total domestic U.S. production and hence the real GDP of the U.S. in the process, it is possible for the U.S. trade deficit to be reduced. The key lies in the increased domestic production to meet the increase in export demand, so that there is a genuine increase in both U.S. real GDP and exports. In the appendix to this chapter, we shall show how an autonomous increase in the demand for exports that is met with new domestic production can reduce the trade deficit of an economy.

The production of new output to meet new autonomous export demands generates new GDP and new employment, making use of the underutilised productive potential in the U.S. What are the examples of such exports? Chicken feet and animal innards, which used to be considered worthless and routinely discarded in the U.S., have found strong demands from China and are exported in bulk. Similarly, waste cardboard paper from used cardboard boxes has also been exported to China to be made into paper pulp, taking advantage of the extremely low freight rates of container ships returning to China with an almost empty load. Other potential U.S. exports from new U.S. production include food and energy products, given the abundant U.S. endowments of land, water and energy resources such as oil and gas, all of which are not fully utilised.

Two sources of potential U.S. exports to China that can be huge and are relatively uncontroversial are agricultural commodities and energy. China has a huge demand for agricultural commodities and, in addition, there is also great potential for the U.S. to increase the value-added content of U.S. agricultural exports, for example, by producing and exporting meat (beef, pork and poultry) instead of feed grains (corn and soybeans) to China.[3] In 2017, China imported more than US$115 billion of agricultural commodities, but only 20 percent of the imports came from the U.S. Moreover,

---

3   In fact, China also stands to gain by importing meat instead of feed grains because of the shortage of fresh water in China. China's per capita fresh water availability is only about 28 percent of the world average, and it is unevenly distributed within the country. Importing directly meat rather than feed grains from the U.S. saves water and can be regarded as an indirect way of importing water.

Chinese imports of agricultural commodities have been increasing by more than 10 percent per year. Thus, there is the potential of U.S. exports of agricultural commodities to China rising from the current US$20 billion plus a year to US$50 billion a year in three to five years, on the basis of new as well as higher value-added U.S. production. The U.S. has significant surplus production capacity (for example, it has an abundance of land, water and pastures) for agricultural commodities if there is assured long-term demand.

China also has a huge and growing demand for energy, especially relatively clean energy, which can be met by exports of liquefied natural gas (from Alaska, for example) and shale oil, which are again new production, from the U.S. In 2016, China imported a total of US$117 billion of crude oil and US$9 billion of natural gas. China's imports of oil and gas from the U.S. were minuscule, at US$0.2 billion and US$0.08 billion respectively. Given China's huge and growing demand for energy, and especially for non-polluting energy such as natural gas, and the U.S. being transformed into a net energy exporter because of its rising shale oil and gas production, it is entirely possible for the U.S. to become a top energy exporter to China, gradually increasing to US$50 billion a year, again based on new production and not the diversion of existing production, thus increasing U.S. GDP and employment.

Thus, it is easy to envisage that additional exports in the agriculture and energy areas alone can amount to US$100 billion a year, with almost 100 percent U.S. value-added content. Moreover, these increased exports are likely to persist for a long time. The beauty of this type of arrangement is that no one is hurt economically. In the U. S., the new exports consist of new domestic supply that already has its committed export demand, so that it will not drive up or drive down prices or otherwise affect the markets. In China, not only are the imports likely to be less expensive than the cost of domestic production on the margin, they serve the important purpose of meeting the expanded and expanding domestic demand, without affecting the prices in the domestic markets. So, all in all, this is likely to be win-win all around.

One may raise the question: if such profitable opportunities for trade exist, why has the trade not occurred already? The answer lies in the fact that the creation of genuine new export supply requires investment, and investment can be justified only if the production (and export) activities can be sustained over time. That is why a new committed long-term demand for the good to be exported is necessary in order that there is new production. However, new long-term demand can arise only if there is new long-term supply, and vice versa. There is therefore the need for the coordination of both the supply and the demand sides. But markets are incomplete, especially futures markets. For example, it is impossible, or prohibitively expensive, to either sell or buy beef or wheat on the futures market for delivery 20 years from the present (actually even three years from now). Thus, one cannot rely on the free markets alone for such long-term trade arrangements involving new supply and demand. Non-market coordination becomes necessary because of the incompleteness of markets.⁴ There must be long-term supply and demand contracts for the new production and export to happen.

For both U.S. producers and Chinese importers, such contracts must be long-term (say, 20 years) and have credible mutually agreeable price-determination and enforcement mechanisms, so that both supplies in the U.S. and demands in China are forthcoming and sustained and not subject to arbitrary interruptions. Whether it is agricultural commodities or energy, only long-term demand contracts can attract U.S. suppliers to make new investments and develop new supplies. And only long-term supply contracts can assure Chinese importers of a dependable, sustainable and uninterruptible supply to meet the domestic demand. Both U.S. suppliers and Chinese importers want a predictable and fair price, determined independently of the spot price, which may fluctuate wildly and is subject to manipulation, so that the U.S. suppliers are assured of a profit and the Chinese importers are assured of affordability. For example, a cost plus price (subject to audit by Chinese importers) that is equal to unit cost plus, say between 5 and 10 percent, may work. This guarantees the U. S. suppliers a profit over the entire period of the supply contract, so that they will have the incentive

---

4   This is no different from the coordination between the establishment of two new enterprises by two different investors, one upstream and one downstream, with the upstream enterprise providing inputs to the downstream enterprise. Without coordination, neither enterprise will be established.

to make the necessary investments. It also protects the Chinese importers against large fluctuations in the prices of the imports, and in particular when the spot price is abnormally high. Without long-term supply contracts, no significant new supply will be forthcoming, and any new Chinese import demand will end up only driving up the prices in the spot market, providing windfall gains to the existing suppliers worldwide without substantively solving the U.S.-China trade deficit problem.

Finally, both food and energy are critical to an economy. For China to rely on imports from the U.S. for 10 percent or more of its food and energy needs on a continuing basis is a major strategic decision. A 10-percent shortfall cannot be easily made whole with purchases from the spot markets. There must be assurances that the supply will not be arbitrarily interrupted. For commercial reasons, U.S. suppliers and Chinese importers will be concerned about the possibility of a ban on U.S. exports to China (that affects either agricultural commodities or energy) imposed by a future U.S. government. They can be protected by, for example, the U.S. exporters/suppliers providing a performance bond in the form of a half-year or one-year physical supply in warehouse facilities in China. If the U.S. suppliers default on the long-term supply contract for whatever reason, including a ban by the U.S. government, the Chinese importer will collect the bond with the contract cancelled simultaneously. With such a provision, a U.S. ban on exports of agricultural commodities or energy to China will have no effect in the short term, and for this reason may never be used, which is exactly what both the U.S. suppliers and Chinese importers want. Even though the transactions are not conducted at prices on the spot market, since the quantities covered by the long-term supply contracts are fixed, they do not affect the efficiency of the free market at all.[5] At the present time, both agricultural and energy exports form the U.S. to China are subject to Chinese tariffs. It is hoped that these tariffs are temporary and that discussions on new long-term supply contracts in the food and energy areas will be resumed in the near future.

---

5   See Lawrence J. Lau, Yingyi Qian and Gerard Roland (2000).

Another fast-growing component of U.S. exports to China is services, also with almost 100 percent value-added content, driven by China's demand for education and tourism.[6] The expenditures of Chinese students and tourists in the U.S. have been rising rapidly. They can also form a significant part of the increase in the U.S. exports of goods and services to China. Actions such as imposing more stringent tourist visa requirements on Chinese tourists and reducing the number of (or banning altogether) visas issued to Chinese students are counter-productive, as they are likely to contribute to widening rather than narrowing the U.S.-China trade deficit.[7] Having more Chinese students and tourists in the U.S. will also help improve the people-to-people relations between the two countries. Moreover, Chinese students who study in the U.S. are among the top one percent of Chinese students. It is an advantage for the U.S. if they stay in the U.S. It will be a good addition to U.S. human capital. It will also be an advantage for the U.S. if they return to China. They will act as goodwill ambassadors for the U.S. Whenever there is a need for something not available in China, the first thought will be to find a supplier in the U.S. Yet it has been reported that the U.S. government considered a blanket ban on all Chinese student visas. If implemented, it would probably reduce the U.S. surplus in trade in services by US$18 billion.[8] Fortunately, the idea seemed to have been shelved for the time being.

All three of the above-mentioned potential areas for increased U.S. exports to China—energy, agricultural commodities, education and tourism services—can contribute significantly to narrowing or even closing the U.S.-China trade deficit in gross value as well as total value-added terms.

Finally, increasing U.S. exports of high-tech goods to China is also a

---

6   The increases in the number of Chinese tourists to the U.S. are due in part to the reciprocal introduction of the ten-year, multiple-entry visa for citizens of each country that was advocated in an earlier study sponsored by the China United States Exchange Foundation (2013) and implemented in 2014.

7   Other U.S. initiatives under consideration include the investigation of researchers and scholars included in China's "Thousand Talents Programme" (千人計劃), a recruitment programme for Chinese scholars overseas to return to China to work either full-time or part-time.

8   *Financial Times* (3 October 2018), p. 1.

possibility, as China's demand for such goods remains high. However, this is likely to be more controversial for national security as well as competitive considerations on the part of the U.S. In addition, for the same reasons that the U.S. government discourages the use of Huawei servers and cell phones in the U.S., the Chinese government may also eventually decide that it is too risky to rely on U.S. high-tech products, such as Apple iPhones. This mutual stand-off is likely to create implicit or even explicit protectionist barriers in both countries, to the benefit of their monopolistic producers and the detriment of their consumers.

A further area of significant potential win-win collaboration is the deployment of the excess Chinese savings in the U.S. for the financing of the renovation and upgrading of U.S. basic infrastructure, as well as the augmentation of the equity capital of U.S. corporations. In addition to the People's Bank of China purchase of U.S. Treasury and Agency securities, Chinese non-governmental institutions and the public at large can also be potential purchasers of bonds for infrastructural projects with their excess savings. U.S. corporations can potentially tap into the Chinese capital market by raising debt and equity there. A useful idea to pursue is for U.S. corporations to issue China Depositary Receipts (CDRs) on the Shanghai Stock Exchange in Renminbi, similar to the American Depositary Receipts (ADRs) of foreign corporations that are traded on U.S. stock exchanges in U.S. Dollars. This can turn out to be win-win as the U.S. corporations will be able to raise additional capital and the Chinese investors have additional avenues to place their savings.

Imports can indeed help to keep the rate of inflation low. Chart 8.1 is a scatter diagram of the annual rate of growth of the U.S. non-oil price index (which is equivalent to the core rate of inflation in the U.S.) versus the Chinese share of U.S. non-oil imports between 1989 and 2017. It is clear that the higher the Chinese share of non-oil imports is, the lower the U.S. core rate of inflation will be. In addition, Lawrence J. Lau and Junjie Tang (2018) have shown that between 1994 and 2017, a one-percentage-point increase in the Chinese share of U.S. non-oil imports reduced the annual rate of growth of the U.S. non-oil price index by 1.0 percentage point. The Chinese share of total U.S. non-oil imports rose more or less continuously from 2.7 percent in 1989 to almost 22 percent in 2009, and then stayed within a narrow range between 21 and 23 percent through 2017. Between 1961 and 1989, the average annual rate of growth of the U.S. non-oil price index was 5.1 percent. Between 1989 and 2017, the average annual rate of growth of the U.S. non-oil price index was only 2.5 percent, a drop of 2.6 percent from the 5.1 percent in the previous 28-year period. The decline in the core rate of inflation, which is essentially the rate of increase of the non-oil price index, since 1989, which has enabled a lower U.S. rate of interest, can be partially attributed to the increase in Chinese imports.[9] Imposing tariffs on Chinese imports will definitely lower its share of U.S. non-oil imports and may raise the U.S. core rate of inflation.

It is indeed difficult to assess which country has benefitted more from their economic relations. China has been able to lift 800 million of its citizens out of poverty, initially through the vast expansion of export-oriented jobs in China that resulted from China's economic opening and accession to the WTO. However, American consumers have benefitted from two decades of low prices of consumer goods. Had U.S. imports from China stayed at 1994 levels, the U.S. Consumer Price Index would have been 27 percent higher in 2017, or approximately one percentage point higher annually. Additional benefits for the U.S. include the profits of U.S. corporations earned by their operations within China, such as General Motors, McDonald's, Starbucks and Walmart, as well as the sales of Apple iPhones, which—since they are assembled within China—are not considered U.S. exports to China.

In addition, if a country can pay for its trade deficit with pieces of paper, such as its currency and bonds which it can print at will at almost zero cost, it can be a huge advantage. And this is what the U.S. has been able to do since the early 1970s, taking advantage of the seigniorage from providing the only widely-accepted international medium of exchange. This benefit has been estimated to be worth as much as US$350 billion a year.

It is actually in the interests of the U.S. to educate and train the future elite of China. It has been a huge advantage for the U.S. to be able to recruit

---

9   See Lawrence J. Lau and Junjie Tang (2018).

Chart 8.1   A Scatter Diagram of the Annual Rate of Growth of the U.S. Non-
            Oil Price Index versus the Chinese Share of U.S. Non-Oil Imports
            (1989–2017)

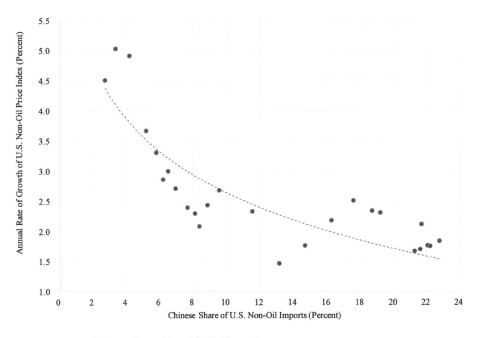

Source: Lawrence J. Lau and Junjie Tang (2018), Chart 15.

the cream of the cream of young people from around the world. All the
other countries feed, educate and nurture their young people until they are
18 years old, and then U.S. universities and colleges can pick off the best.
Foreign students are a boon for the U.S., especially at the graduate level.
In the natural sciences and engineering departments of many of the most
elite universities in the U.S., most of the graduate students in their Ph.D.
programmes, who also work as research or teaching assistants, come from
China, India and Russia. If no foreign graduate students are admitted, these
departments will not have enough students or assistants.

    In conclusion, I believe the U.S.-China trade deficit, estimated to
be US$111 billion in total value-added terms, can be closed by the U.S.
increasing its exports to China in agricultural commodities, energy and

services on a long-term basis. Given the rising demands in China and the potential new supplies available in the U.S., such increased long-term trade should be beneficial to both economies and will deepen their mutual economic interdependence. Moreover, while these benefits will represent net gains to both economies as both the supplies and the demands do not exist before, they are unlikely to affect the existing participants in the markets for agricultural commodities and energy since their transactions will take place away from the spot markets.

Appendix

We shall show how an autonomous increase in the demand for exports that is met with new domestic production can reduce the trade deficit. The national income identity of an economy may be written as:

$$Y = C + I + G + X - M,$$

where Y is the aggregate real output of an economy (real GDP), C is real personal consumption, I is real gross investment, G is real government consumption, X is real exports and M is real imports, and $X - M$ is the trade surplus or deficit. The savings of the economy, the difference between output and consumption, is given by:

$$S = Y - (C + G) = I + X - M,$$

which may be rewritten as:

$$I - S = M - X,$$

that is, the excess of investment over savings is the difference between imports and exports, which is precisely the trade deficit/surplus, for a given aggregate real output Y. It is in this sense that the aggregate trade deficit with the rest of the world is determined by $I - S$, the difference between domestic real investment and domestic real savings, or equivalently, the investment-savings balance. The trade deficit (which can be negative, in which case it is a surplus) is precisely equal to the excess of domestic investment over domestic savings.

To see how an autonomous (unanticipated) increase in exports, based on underutilised domestic resources, can reduce the trade deficit, suppose the increase is represented by DX, which in turn generates an increase in Y of DY. The increase in real GDP (DY) may generate an increase in personal consumption (DC), which must in any case be less than DY, but it should not generate any increase in government consumption (G), at least not until the following budget cycle, and in imports (M). It may, however, require a small increase in investment (I). The change in domestic savings is given by:

$$\Delta S = \Delta Y - \Delta C = \Delta I + \Delta X, \text{ so that:}$$

$$\Delta S - \Delta I = \Delta X,$$

which is greater than zero since there is an increase in exports. The difference between investment and savings, $(I + \Delta I) - (S + \Delta S) = I - S - (\Delta S - \Delta I) = I - S - \Delta X$, is therefore reduced and the trade deficit is also reduced correspondingly. This can happen because there is pre-existing surplus potential output, which can be produced with relatively few additional inputs, and then exported.

Part III

Beyond the Trade War

9. The Long-Term Forces at Work

It is important to realise that behind the current China-U.S. trade war, there are two important long-term developments simultaneously in play in China-U.S. economic relations. The first has to do with the competition between major world powers, and the second has to do with the rise of populist, isolationist, nationalist and protectionist sentiments in the world and in particular in the U.S.

First, one of the principal causes of the current trade war between China and the U.S. is actually not trade itself, but the potential competition between the two nations for economic and technological dominance. This competition, whether explicit or implicit, and whether intentional or not, did not begin with President Donald Trump and is not going away even after President Trump leaves office. The "pivot to Asia" and the "Trans-Pacific Partnership" (TPP), both policies supposedly meant to contain or restrain China's development, were initiated under President Barack Obama (but seemingly abandoned by President Trump).

Comparison between China and the U.S., and hence implicit competition between the two major world powers, is probably unavoidable. However, the competition can potentially lead to constructive and positive as well as destructive and negative outcomes. As mentioned in Chapter 7, competition has already resulted in both China and the U.S. producing better and faster super-computers.

However, the targets of competition must be chosen carefully. There is of course no point in China and the U.S. competing in terms of total population. In fact, even China long ago resigned to ceding the top position in the world's population to India by the mid-2030s. In terms of aggregate GDP, China went from only 20 percent of the U.S. GDP in 2000 to two-thirds in 2017.

The world's second largest economy has been growing too fast for the comfort of the largest economy. It is probably only a matter of time before China's GDP catches up with the U.S. GDP, given its much larger population (1.42 billion versus 327 million) and much higher average annual rate of growth (6 percent versus 3 percent), probably in the 2030s.[1]

However, in terms of GDP per capita, China is still way behind, with US\$9,137, not even one-sixth of US\$59,518 of the U.S. in 2017. My own projections suggest that it will probably take until the end of the 21st century before China's GDP per capita approaches the U.S. level, if it does at all.

In terms of the number of nuclear-armed warheads, I believe the U.S. is already way ahead by at least an order of magnitude or two in total and even more in per capita terms. This is not a competition that China should wish to join. However, a race to find an effective cure for cancer or Alzheimer's disease would be worthwhile for both countries and in fact for all of humankind.

The economic competition has led to complaints about the exchange rate of the Renminbi (too low because of alleged manipulation), the lack of market access to China for U.S. firms, the perceived favouritism for China's SOEs, and the industrial policy of the Chinese government. The competition for technological dominance has bred grievances on the part of the U.S. on inadequate intellectual property rights protection, forced transfer of technology and cyber-theft of commercial and industrial information. (Note that none of these complaints and grievances have much to do directly with trade or tariffs per se.) These grievances culminated in the decision of President Trump to impose three separate rounds of new U.S. tariffs on

---

1   According to the IMF and the World Bank, China's economy is already the largest in the world in "purchasing-power-parity" terms. I personally do not believe that being number one in aggregate GDP is that important. A much more important indicator of relative strength is GDP per capita. Scientific, technological and military capabilities are also much more important than aggregate GDP.

imports from China of cumulatively US$250 billion worth in 2018, starting a trade war between the two countries.

Although market access and forced technology transfer are related, they are actually separate issues. While it is indeed true that the Chinese economy can become even more open on international trade with and direct investment from the rest of the world, it has been and still is much more open than either Japan or South Korea at a comparable stage of development. For example, many foreign automobile manufacturers such as Germany's BMW and Volkswagen, the U.S.'s General Motors and Ford, and Japan's Honda and Toyota, have highly successful and profitable joint-venture manufacturing operations in China. Fast food and coffee outlets such as McDonald's and Starbucks, and retail stores like Walmart, are ubiquitous in China. There is a large presence of foreign financial services firms in China. This was not the case in either Japan or South Korea at the comparable stages of their development.

China maintains restrictions on foreign direct investment (FDI) in certain sectors. These restrictions are mostly designed to protect the domestic enterprises. However, after 40 years of economic reform, many Chinese enterprises have become both large and strong, and it is no longer justifiable to invoke the "infant industry" argument in favour of protection. But restrictions on foreign ownership are not uncommon in many other countries. For example, the U.S. does not permit a foreign investor to own more than 25 percent of a U.S. airline. Neither Japan nor South Korea has allowed wholly-foreign-owned automobile manufacturing operations. (In fact, there are very few foreign joint ventures in the automobile manufacturing industry in these two countries.) In addition, foreign investment into the U.S. may need to be approved by the CFIUS, which has broad discretionary powers. Complete liberalisation of FDI into China is probably difficult to achieve in the short run. A framework that involves separate and different negative lists for FDI and national treatment otherwise on a reciprocal basis appears to be the best way forward. The new, much-shortened negative list on FDI announced recently should help.

Intellectual property protection in China has also been vastly improved since special intellectual property courts were set up in Beijing, Shanghai and Guangzhou in 2014.[2] Economically meaningful fines have begun to be levied on violators of intellectual property rights in China. It is considered a fundamental property right for an individual or a firm to protect their core knowledge or technology. This was certainly the case in the old days in China, when masters would withhold their core competence from most apprentices except for their own direct lineal male descendants. As the Chinese begin to innovate on their own, they themselves will demand that intellectual property rights protection be strengthened in China. Japan and Taiwan, in their respective early stages of economic development, also did little to protect intellectual property rights. But as they changed from being a user and imitator to a creator of intellectual property, they began to vigorously enforce intellectual property rights. Now that the Chinese are becoming innovators and inventors themselves, intellectual property rights protection in China should get even better over time.

Technological competition is motivated by commercial as well as national security considerations. No individual or firm will want to give away or sell its core competences. It should therefore not be surprising that nations, firms and individuals will all want to protect their core competences. In the case of the atomic bomb, the former Soviet Union developed it independently without any assistance from the U.S.; China developed it independently without any foreign assistance; France developed its "force de frappe" independently; India, Pakistan and even North Korea developed their nuclear capabilities independently. China will have to develop its own advanced semiconductor, artificial intelligence and aircraft industries, as it may not be able to import the best available from other countries.

China and the U.S. are the two largest markets in the world. As such, most discoverers and inventors would want to register their patents in both China and the U.S. Both countries should facilitate the application for pat-

---

2   This is one of the policy measures advocated by the China–United States Exchange Foundation (2013) and adopted by the Chinese government. In fact, the Ministry of Commerce of the People's Republic of China revealed that Chinese enterprises paid almost US$30 billion in intellectual property royalties to U.S. companies in 2017 (*Financial Times*, 16 July 2018, p. 4). However, part of these payments may show up as service income received by Ireland or the Netherlands subsidiaries of U.S. companies instead of the U.S. companies themselves.

ents by nationals of each in the other's jurisdiction. It is probably unrealistic to expect reciprocal recognition of each other's patent grants. However, it is possible to arrange for the recognition and acceptance of work papers submitted to support the patent application in one country to be used in the patent application process in the other country. This should greatly expedite the patent application process. Moreover, both governments can agree to charge lower renewal fees for patents granted on a reciprocal basis.

Forced technology transfer has to do with China's requirements for foreign direct investors in certain industries to take Chinese enterprises as equal joint-venture partners. For example, a foreign automobile manufacturer used to have to form a joint venture with a Chinese enterprise as a partner in order to establish a manufacturing operation in China and could only own up to 50 percent of the joint venture. It is perfectly understandable that a firm like General Motors may not want to share trade secrets with a potential competitor. However, the sharing of technology in a joint venture is a voluntary one. The foreign direct investor will have to weigh the benefits of having a local joint-venture partner versus the costs. In any case, the technology used in the current manufacturing process is probably already on the way to becoming obsolete. What is more valuable is the next-generation technology that has yet to be implemented. This is what the foreign direct investor can still maintain as its own in its home factories and laboratories.

The situation has, however, been changed recently. For many industries, a joint-venture partner is no longer required, and the restriction on the percentage of foreign ownership has been lifted. For example, in the automobile manufacturing industry, Tesla has been able to establish a wholly-owned subsidiary in Shanghai to manufacture electric cars. BMW, Germany's automobile manufacturer, has been allowed to increase its equity stake in BMW Brilliance Automotive Company—its joint venture in Shenyang, China—to 75 percent from 50 percent, by paying its joint-venture partner, Brilliance China Automotive Holdings Ltd., approximately US$4 billion. Even though it is now possible for General Motors to buy out its Chinese joint-venture partner in Shanghai, it has indicated that it does not intend to do so. This issue of forced technology transfer has now become mostly moot, as joint ventures are no longer required of foreign direct investors by the Chinese government in many industries. In addition, there have also been significant liberalisation measures in the financial sector. Foreign investors are allowed to own more than 50 percent of a financial services company and up to 100 percent in three years' time.

Cyber-theft is an issue that requires collaboration and cooperation of both governments. The solution should be a vigorous prosecution of the criminal perpetrators on both sides. I believe instances of state-sanctioned commercial cyber-theft are rare, even though state-sponsored espionage is a game played by every major country since time immemorial. The Chinese government does not condone the theft of intellectual property (in fact, theft of any kind), nor does it engage in cyber-theft itself. This is clear from its establishment of a special intellectual property court system that has jurisdiction of the entire country. However, one cannot rule out freelancers being engaged and financed by private individuals and firms to engage in cyber-theft. The obvious and straightforward solution is for the victims of such thefts to produce credible evidence, file formal complaints against the wrongdoers and request the Chinese government to assist in the investigation. Even if an SOE is involved, charges should still be pressed and investigated—the perpetrators need to be identified and prosecuted.

Trade in high-tech products and in technology itself, including cross-border investment in high-tech firms, will probably remain problematic as long as there are considerations of both technological competition and national security. For the same national security reasons as the U.S. government discourages the use of Huawei servers and cell phones in the U.S., the Chinese government may also eventually decide that it is risky to rely on U.S. high-tech products. It is interesting to note that mobile telephones, which include Apple iPhones[3], are exempted from the list of China's export products subject to the new U.S. tariffs. The potential mutual stand-off is likely to lead to explicit or implicit protection in both countries, to the benefit of their respective domestic monopolistic producers. But it will also encourage and incentivise indigenous technological development.

---

3   China's domestic value-added content on the Apple iPhone is probably no more than 5 percent of its gross value.

"Made in China, 2025", an initiative of China to move up the industrial value chain, becomes even more urgent and necessary.

The rise of populist, isolationist, nationalist and protectionist sentiments in the U.S. and elsewhere in the world will also have significant impacts on international trade and investment (and migration). President Trump did not create these sentiments, but he has been able to tap into them and exploit them very effectively. The root cause is that while economic globalisation (and innovation) have benefitted all countries in the world, including both China and the U.S., the economic benefits have not been widely shared within each country, resulting in the emergence of winners and losers. In principle, there is sufficient overall gain to be shared so that no one needs to lose, but the free market alone cannot and will not make it happen. Thus, there are people who have been left behind and whose well-being has not improved for the past two, three or even four decades. In the meantime, the income distribution has become more unequal in every country, in part because of the super-low rates of interest created by the various central banks of developed economies. The losers believe that the government and the elite establishment have failed them and are eager to try something else, anything. It is easy to lay the blame on globalisation, in other words, on foreigners, and become isolationist and protectionist. It is up to the government of each country to take care of its domestic losers, who instinctively and naturally oppose economic globalisation and free trade.

What is "Fair" Trade?

When is trade considered fair? While the theory of comparative advantage shows that both trading-partner countries benefit in the aggregate if they trade, it does not specify how the gains from trade are to be distributed between them. The relative distribution of gains depends on their initial positions, comparative advantages and relative market power. There is no generally accepted simple indicator or yardstick for the degree of fairness, which remains a subjective concept.

One possible notion of "fairness" could be a bilateral trade balance of zero. But this notion of fairness does not make too much economic sense.

For example, it will require a major oil exporter such as Saudi Arabia to have balanced trade with every other country, large and small. Another possible notion of "fairness" is a trade balance of zero with the rest of the world. While this may seem fair enough, it will in actuality deprive the U.S. of the opportunity to benefit from the seigniorage of providing the world with an international medium of exchange. The U.S. runs a large trade deficit with the rest of the world. It pays for its excess imports with U.S. Dollars or U.S. Dollar–denominated bonds, both of which it can print more or less at will. Most of the rest of the world is content to keep the U.S. Dollars and bonds as part of their official foreign exchange reserves, which is needed to support its international transactions. In fact, one can argue that if the U.S. does not run a trade deficit with the world, there may not be sufficient U.S. Dollar liquidity (international money) to support all the international transactions in the world. So, the U.S. provides an important and useful service to the world by supplying a widely accepted international medium of exchange. However, the ability of the U.S. to maintain a persistent trade deficit with the rest of the world can also be regarded as an advantage rather than a disadvantage for the U.S. Basically it means the U.S. can buy things with virtually unlimited credit, as long as the rest of the world is willing to indefinitely hold U.S. Dollars and bonds.

Still another notion of fairness is that all trading-partner countries should be treated identically—be charged the same price, be subject to the same tariffs and quotas, etc.—so that there is no discriminatory treatment. In practice, there is discriminatory treatment almost everywhere because of bilateral or multilateral trade agreements of various kinds.

China has been a major beneficiary of economic globalisation. By opening its economy and acceding to the WTO, it has managed to grow to be the second largest economy in the world as well as the second largest trading nation. More than 800 million Chinese people have been lifted out of poverty over the past four decades. None of this would have been possible had China not decided to undertake economic reform and join the world economy in 1978. The U.S. may feel that China has benefitted much more than the U.S. and therefore the outcome is "unfair". Some Chinese people also feel that since much of China's exports of goods to the rest of the world have actually been produced by foreign-owned or joint-venture enterprises, many of which have U.S. corporate parents, it is unfair to attribute the gains from the "trade surplus" to China. Still China's another complaint is the low domestic value-added content of some of China's exports, which has already been discussed. In any case, it is difficult to quantify and compare the benefits that each country derives from trade, especially since the perceived benefits and costs may be different for different countries. And there is no compelling economic logic why the benefits, even if measurable, should be the same among trading-partner countries, and how the distribution of the benefits can be made more "fair".

Finally, it should be recognised that the market does not concern itself with "fairness". Any voluntary and non-coercive trade between a willing buyer and a willing seller at the market price can and should be considered "fair".

In addition, it is natural and instinctive for any individual to entertain the feeling of "us" versus "them". And most people believe that all deals are zero-sum, that is, "more for them is less for us, and vice versa". It is therefore a revelation to many that voluntary trade between two countries benefits both, that is, it is in fact win-win. Unfortunately, it will take a while before the people at large realise that protectionism is a lose-lose proposition. The eventual solution has to be some form of redistribution within each coun-try—taxing the winners to compensate the losers so that everyone wins.

President Trump also believes that every deal is zero sum—one country's gain must be another country's loss. Moreover, he would like to modify the existing distribution of gains from trade between the U.S. and its trading-partner countries. He believes that the U.S. can achieve much better trade deals by negotiating bilaterally with every single country and taking full advantage of the market size and bargaining power of the U.S., including the fact that typically the U.S. Dollar has to be used as an inter-national medium of exchange by every country. President Trump would like to modify the existing distribution of gains from trade between the U.S. and its trading-partner countries and believes that this would work the best in a bilateral rather than multilateral context.[4]

---

4   More simply put, a large country does not have to be a price-taker internationally.

A New Type of Major-Power Relation

On 10 June 2013, at the presidential summit between former U.S. President
Barack Obama and Chinese President Xi Jinping in Sunnylands, California, President Xi first proposed the idea of a "New Type of Major-Power
Relation" as a new framework for the conduct of future bilateral relations
between China and the U.S. It essentially suggests the following:

First, both China and the U.S. should maintain a close dialogue with
each other and avoid conflict or confrontation.

Second, both countries should treat each other as a peer[5] and respect
each other, including each other's core interests and major concerns.

Third, both countries should engage in mutually beneficial cooperation, develop a win-win relationship and advance areas of common interest.

The proposal for a new type of major-power relation may be understood
as a continuation of China's "peaceful development" (previously known as
"peaceful rise") policy, promoted by former Chinese President Hu Jintao. Its
aim is to avoid open conflict or confrontation, or a cold or hot war with the
U.S. as China continues to develop and grow.

This type of major-power relation—a mutually beneficial, cooperative
and respectful friendly relationship based on genuine equality—is indeed
new not only to the world but also to both China and the U.S. To advance
to this new type of major-power relation, a reset of the existing China-U.S.
relation is involved because up to the present time this has not been quite
the mode in which the bilateral relationship has been conducted. The U.S.
has been a mentor to China in its transition from a centrally planned economy to a market economy, albeit one with Chinese characteristics, and a
model for its economic development. The U.S. has been a major power since
the early 20th century and has been recognised as such by all. China has only
recently become a major power, despite having been one of the five countries
with a permanent seat in the United Nations Security Council since the
establishment of the United Nations. The new type of major-power relation

---

5   The term "near-peer" is sometimes used by U.S. commentators in reference to China.
     But "near-peer" is not the same as "peer". It is not a relationship on an equal footing.

implies that the U.S. and China will accord each other the courtesy and respect of not only a friendly but also an equal power.

When China first began its economic reform and opening to the world, almost every type of inbound FDI was welcome. A major mandatory task of all local officials in those days was the generation of foreign exchange. Their individual job performance was judged on the basis of the quantity of real GDP, employment and foreign exchange that each of them was able to create. At one time, inbound FDI constituted almost 20 percent of total gross domestic fixed investment in the Chinese economy. At the time, all important visiting foreign businessmen were treated like royalty by the officials of the central and local governments because they were all considered to be potential direct investors. From the beginning of the economic reform and opening to the world in 1978, up to 10 to 15 years ago, it was routine for the Chairmen and/or CEO of major U.S. corporations such as AIG, Chase Manhattan Bank, General Motors, HSBC and IBM to be personally received by either the General Secretary of the Communist Party of China or by the Premier of the State Council of the People's Republic of China in Beijing. However, as the Chinese economy prospered, its aggregate and per capita GDP grew, its own manufacturing industries gained in both size and sophistication, and its trade surplus and foreign exchange reserves increased, the importance of inbound FDI gradually declined. In 2017, the share of FDI in total Chinese gross domestic fixed investment fell below 1.4 percent and China's official foreign exchange reserves were the world's largest, exceeding US$3 trillion! FDI would no longer be important from either a macroeconomic or balance of payments viewpoint but would still be welcome if it would bring technology, new business models and access to markets that China otherwise would not have.[6] China has also been gradually transformed from "the world's factory" to "the world's market". More and more direct investors want to sell things to China rather than to make things in China for export.

---

6   The truth is that the Chinese economy is awash in surplus savings. To be successful in China, a foreign direct investor must be able to bring to China more than just capital.

Today, it would be rare for a foreign corporate chieftain to have a private audience with a Chinese senior leader. This is not unique to American tycoons; it is also true for tycoons from all foreign countries, and from Hong Kong, Macau and Taiwan. It reflects the change in China's priorities and the relative bargaining power between the Chinese government and foreign direct investors. The Chinese side is able to strike a harder bargain than before. What one would be willing to give when the real GDP per capita was US$383, as in China of 1978, would be very different from when the GDP per capita grew to US$9,137 (in 2017 prices). Some adjustments in attitudes and behaviour on the part of both sides would be justifiable. This applies to not only negotiations between enterprises but also negotiations between governments.

Moreover, neither China nor the U.S. really know how to treat another country as an equal peer—neither of them have had any experience of treating a friendly nation as a genuine equal. Historically, China either treated all other countries as vassal states, especially when it was rich and strong, or it was subservient to the more powerful foreign nations (for example, Western nations between 1840 and 1949 and Japan from the late 19th century up to the Sino-Japanese War during 1937–1945). The U.S. was minimally involved in the world at large in the 19th century, except for the promulgation and implementation of the Monroe Doctrine, effectively closing the Western Hemisphere to further colonisation by European powers. The U.S. certainly has no peer in both North and South America. The U.S. was a saviour to the U.K., France and other countries in Western Europe in the two World Wars. It was a victor to (and one-time occupier of) Germany, Italy and Japan. It was the mainstay of the North Atlantic Treaty Organisation (NATO) and defended Western Europe from Soviet expansionism between 1945 and 1989 and since then from Russia. It fought to preserve South Korea in the Korean War. It still maintains troops in Japan and South Korea, helping to defend them and providing a nuclear umbrella. The U.S. considers all of these countries to be friends, but fundamentally does not consider any of them to be an equal. They may even be allies, but peers they are not. The U.S. did consider the former Soviet Union as an equal, but it was not a friend; it was an adversary.

Both China and the U.S. also believe that each of them is "exceptional", sometimes meaning that conventional rules that apply to all the other countries in the world do not apply to them. The unilateral U.S. withdrawal from the Bretton-Woods system of fixed exchange rates among nations in 1971 is such an example. The U.S. is frequently in arrears on the payment of its dues to the United Nations, one time for as long as 20 years. More recently, the threat by the U.S. of sanctions against foreign firms that will continue to trade with Iran after the U.S. withdrawal from the Joint Comprehensive Plan of Action of the Iran nuclear deal is another example.[7] China refused to accept the decision of the Arbitral Tribunal for the South China Sea Arbitration in 2016, justifying it on the basis that "the Tribunal's many errors deprive its awards of validity".[8] However, in the years ahead, both China and the U.S. have to try to learn to treat each other as an equal friend and respect and accept each other's differences. In particular, they have to respect each other's core interests and accept that each other is also "exceptional" in its own way. For example, the "reunification of Taiwan with China" is central to the Chinese renaissance. Any action taken towards the independence of Taiwan is a red line for China. Similarly, Latin America is and remains the exclusive backyard of the U.S. China also wants to evolve in its own way as a polity and society, without causing any harm to other countries, and it hopes that its right to do so will be respected.

However, as our analyses in the chapters above indicate, China and the U.S. will not be equal in many respects for a long time. While in the aggregate, China's real GDP may exceed U.S. real GDP in, say, another 15 years, China's real GDP per capita will not catch up to U.S. real GDP per capita until the end of the 21st century at the earliest. China will also lag behind the U.S. in science and technology for at least a couple of decades. China's military capability will be sufficient as a deterrent but not sufficient to threaten the U.S. for a long time to come. However, China would like to be treated with the courtesy accorded to an equal friend or an equal partner,

---

7   Iran is not under sanctions mandated by the United Nations as North Korea is.
8   See Chinese Society of International Law (June 2018)

even though they are not really equal as yet. Perhaps in the future, it will be treated as a peer, with equality, by the U.S. However, it is definitely too early to speak of China and the U.S. as being a "Group of Two" or "G-2".

China and the U.S. are not predestined to be foes. China does not have any intention to dominate the world. It is inevitable that China's real GDP will eventually surpass the U.S. real GDP, given the size of China's population. But that alone should not be a cause for war. Whether China and the U.S. will become friends or foes in the future depends on the expectations on both sides, which can be self-fulfilling. If they both believe that they will be friends and act accordingly, they will be friends; if they both believe that they will be foes and act accordingly, they will become foes. Thus, expectations must be carefully managed by the leaders on both sides, building friendship and mutual trust between the two peoples.

Professor Graham Allison of the Kennedy School at Harvard University has written about the inevitability of a China-U.S. war.[9] As a rising power challenges the dominance of an established power, the established power is likely to respond with force. He refers to this "inevitability" as the "Thucydides Trap", drawing on Thucydides's *History of the Peloponnesian War*. However, a war between China and the U.S. is far from inevitable. This is because such a war is likely to result in not only a completely devastated China but also the destruction of one or two major U.S. cities along with their populations. There will be no real winners. It would just be pure madness. The U.S. is obviously the stronger military power and has the capacity to launch a first strike. That is why China must at all times maintain the capability for a minimum level of deterrence so as to discourage a hostile attack. What is more important and effective is to increase mutual economic interdependence between China and the U.S. to make a war totally unthinkable.

---

9   See Graham T. Allison (2015).

10. The Way Forward

In this concluding chapter, I would like to provide a brief summary of what we have done in this book. First of all, exports contribute to an economy through the GDP and employment that they create domestically. The magnitude of their benefits depends on the domestic value-added (profits, salaries and wages) that they generate and not on the gross value of the exports themselves. Thus, in comparing the relative benefits of the bilateral trade between two countries, we should focus on the total value-added (GDP) created, not on the gross value.[1] In Chapter 3, we have reconstructed the estimate of the U.S.-China trade deficit and shown that in total value-added (or GDP) terms, it was only US$111 billion in 2017, compared to the often-quoted figure of US$376 billion in terms of the gross value of the goods exported. It is completely feasible for the U.S. to increase its exports to China by US$111 billion in total value-added terms, which would be approximately equivalent to US$125 billion in gross-value terms, given the high domestic value-added content of actual and potential U.S. exports to China.

Second, in Chapter 4, we have shown that the real impacts of the China-U.S. trade war in 2018 will result in at most a 1.12-percent reduction in China's GDP, assuming that half of China's exports of goods to the U.S. are halted by the new U.S. tariffs. This is relatively insignificant and manageable for China, which has an average annual rate of growth of 6.5 percent. The real impacts on the U.S. economy are even less, resulting in a

---

1   The Apple iPhone is an example of a product exported by China which has a high gross value but a very low domestic value-added content, estimated to be around 4 percent.

potential reduction of at most 0.30 percent in the U.S. GDP, compared to its average annual long-term rate of growth of approximately 3 percent. The trade war does have psychological effects that are negative on the Chinese stock markets and the exchange rate of the Renminbi. However, these effects are likely to be transitory.

Third, we have also analysed the potential economic and technological competition between China and the U.S. and the rise of populist, isolationist, nationalist and protectionist sentiments around the world, in particular in the U.S., that lie behind the trade war. The implicit competition between China and the U.S. to be the largest economy in the world, as well as competition in the core technologies of the 21st century, probably cannot be avoided. However, even though China's aggregate real GDP is likely to surpass the U.S. aggregate real GDP sometime in the 2030s, our analysis shows that China still remains far, far behind in terms of real GDP per capita, and will only be able to catch up by the very end of the 21st century. Moreover, in terms of the level of scientific and technological development and innovative capacity, China still has at least a couple of decades to go before it can catch up to the overall level of the U.S. As to the potential xenophobia in both countries, it is up to each government to demonstrate not only by words but also by actions that there is sufficiently large gain in each country for everyone to win with further and closer international economic cooperation, especially long-term multilateral economic cooperation.

Fourth, we have shown in Chapter 8 that China-U.S. economic collaboration and cooperation can result in a win-win for both China and the U.S. Given the economic complementarities between the two countries, both can benefit significantly by enabling the fuller utilisation of the resources in both countries—for example, the energy, land and water resources in the U.S., and the human resources and savings in China—through mutual trade and investment. Moreover, it is entirely feasible for the two countries to achieve essentially long-term balanced trade in goods and services bilaterally within five years if they work together. We have outlined a way forward for narrowing the U.S.-China trade deficit, with significant benefits for both China and the U.S., and positive spillover effects for the rest of the world. It deserves to be seriously considered by both countries. Furthermore, through undertaking projects that enhance mutual long-term economic interdependence between the two countries, mutual trust will grow and the probability of potential conflict between the two countries can be significantly reduced.

The competition between China and the U.S., whether friendly or unfriendly, can be assumed to be an ongoing and long-term one. It will be the "new normal". The trade dispute is only a symptom of the potential possible conflicts between the two countries. There is also the possibility that the competition can become ideological. However, it is unlikely that China will want to convert the U.S. to its system of governance. It is also unlikely for the U.S. to succeed in converting China to the U.S. system of governance. The Chinese people will probably never become as individualistic as the Americans. Democracy will probably evolve in a different way in China compared to the U.S. and take a different form, for cultural, historical and path-dependent reasons. What both countries should and can also do is learn to accept and live with each other's peculiarities and feelings of exceptionalism.

Public enterprises are viewed more positively in China than in the U.S. China's SOEs are unlikely to disappear soon. What private enterprises in both countries should demand is not so much ownership reform or privatisation of China's SOEs, but national treatment in each other, except possibly for national security considerations. National treatment means that a U.S. enterprise operating in China will be treated in the same way as a Chinese enterprise, and vice versa. However, just because an enterprise is state-owned, it does not imply that the state is responsible for all of its behaviour and actions. The state is only one of many shareholders. One cannot simply blame the shareholders and hold them responsible for the behaviour and actions of enterprises in which they have invested. For example, Uber shareholders cannot be held responsible for what Uber does, but the board of directors and the senior management of Uber can and should be.

In addition to the China-U.S. trade war, there appear to be trade wars everywhere: between the U.S. and Canada and Mexico (which apparently has been settled), between the U.S. and the European Union, between the U.S. and Japan, etc. It is difficult to predict how these trade wars will end up. China and the rest of the world, except possibly the U.S., will probably continue to uphold the current multilateral trading system under the WTO among themselves. After all, they have all benefitted and will continue to benefit from it.

This is actually the time for China to continue opening its economy to both international trade and investment, inbound as well as outbound. It can lower tariffs unilaterally, on automobile imports for example, to all countries not at a trade war with China. It can grant and receive privileges on trade and investment to and from all countries on a reciprocal basis. It should understand that international trade and cross-border direct investment are always win-win, and that competition, both domestic and international, improves efficiency and encourages innovation. It should therefore try to be as inclusive as possible in terms of its international economic relations. However, China-U.S. relations are concerned with more than just economics and must be carefully managed by the leaders of both countries going forward.

* * * * *

I was born in China towards the end of World War II. I grew up in Hong Kong and went to the U.S. for college in 1961. I began my long teaching career as an economist at Stanford University in 1966. In 2004, I moved back to Hong Kong to assume the position of the President of The Chinese University of Hong Kong.

I visited China for the first time as an adult in 1979, soon after China decided to undertake economic reform and open its economy to the world, as a member of a delegation of the American Economic Association, led by the late Professor Lawrence R. Klein, a Nobel Laureate in Economic Sciences. At the end of the delegation's visit, we were asked to forecast the rate of growth of the Chinese economy. Using a simple supply-side econometric model that I had built, I forecast 8 percent, the highest in our delegation. As it turned out, the average annual rate of growth of the Chinese economy over the past 40 years was almost 10 percent. I have been involved in advising China's economic policy-makers since that first visit.

The year 2018 marks the 40th anniversary of China's economic reform and opening. It has been 40 years of extraordinary success. China's success owed a great deal to the advice and assistance of many Americans over the years. For example, Professor Klein served as an Adviser to the State Planning Commission of China for US$1 a year; Professor Joseph E. Stiglitz, another Nobel Laureate in Economic Sciences, has been and still is a frequent visitor to China and an adviser to its senior leaders.

China and the U.S. are not predestined to be enemies. They can be simultaneously strategic competitors and collaborative partners. The world is large enough for both of them to continue to grow and prosper, and to collaborate and cooperate with each other for their mutual benefit and for the welfare of the entire world. I am both hopeful and optimistic that China and the U.S. will find a way to work together again not only for their common good, but also for all mankind.

Bibliography

Allison, Graham T. "The Thucydides Trap: Are the U.S. and China Headed for War?" *The Atlantic*, 24 September 2015.

Chen, Xikang, Leonard K. Cheng, K. C. Fung and Lawrence J. Lau. "The Estimation of Domestic Value-Added and Employment Induced by Exports: An Application to Chinese Exports to the United States." In Yin-Wong Cheung and Kar-Yiu Wong, eds., *China and Asia: Economic and Financial Interactions*. Oxon: Routledge, 2009, pp. 64–82.

Chen, Xikang, Leonard K. Cheng, K. C. Fung, Lawrence J. Lau, Yun-Wing Sung, Kunfu Zhu, Cuihong Yang, Jiansuo Pei and Yuwen Duan. "Domestic Value Added and Employment Generated by Chinese Exports: A Quantitative Estimation." *China Economic Review* 23 (April 2012), pp. 850–864.

Chen, Xikang, Lawrence J. Lau, Junjie Tang and Yanyan Xiong. "New and Revised Estimates of the China-U.S. Trade Balance." Working Paper, Lau Chor Tak Institute of Global Economics and Finance, The Chinese University of Hong Kong, 2018.

Chen, Xikang and Huijuan Wang. *Touru zhanyong chanchu jishu* 投入佔用產出技術 (Input-output-occupancy techniques). Beijing: Scientific Publishing Co., 2016.

China–United States Exchange Foundation. *U.S.-China in 2022: U.S.-China Economic Relations in the Next Ten Years—Towards Deeper Engagement and Mutual Benefit*. Hong Kong: China–United States Exchange Foundation, 2013.

Chinese Society of International Law. *Chinese Journal of International Law, Special Issue: The South China Sea Arbitration Awards: A Critical Study* 17, no. 2 (1 June 2018), pp. 207–748. https://doi.org/10.1093/chinesejil/jmy012.

Fung, Kwok-Chiu and Lawrence J. Lau. "The China–United States Bilateral Trade Balance: How Big Is It Really?" *Pacific Economic Review* 3, no. 1 (February 1998), pp. 33–47.

———. "New Estimates of the United States–China Bilateral Trade Balances." *Journal of the Japanese and International Economies* 15, no. 1 (March 2001), pp. 102–130.

Fung, Kwok-Chiu, Lawrence J. Lau and Yanyan Xiong. "Adjusted Estimates of United States–China Bilateral Trade Balances: An Update." *Pacific Economic Review* 11, no. 3 (October 2006), pp. 299–314.

Krugman, Paul. "Increasing Returns, Monopolistic Competition and International Trade." *Journal of International Economics*, November 1979, pp. 469–479.

Kynge, James. "China's Climb to Tech Supremacy is Unstoppable." *Financial Times*, 24 August 2018.

Lampton, David M. "A New Type of Major-Power Relationship: Seeking a Durable Foundation for U.S.-China Ties." *Asia Policy* 16 (July 2013), pp. 51–68.

Lau, Lawrence J. "The Use of Purchasing-Power-Parity Exchange Rates in Economic Modeling." Working Paper, Department of Economics, The Chinese University of Hong Kong, 2007.

———. "A Better Alternative to a Trade War." *China and the World: Ancient and Modern Silk Road* 1, no. 2 (June 2018), pp. 1850014-1–1850014-13.

———. "China's Economic Transition and Outward Direct Investments." In Xuedong Ding and Chen Meng, eds., *From World Factory to Global Investor: A Multi-Perspective Analysis on China's Outward Direct Investment*. London: Taylor and Francis Group / Routledge, 2018 (a), pp. 37–45.

———. "The Chinese Economy in the New Era." Working Paper No. 69, Lau Chor Tak Institute of Global Economics and Finance, The Chinese University of Hong Kong, 2018 (b).

———. "The Sky Is Not Falling! (III)." Working Paper No. 70, Lau Chor Tak Institute of Global Economics and Finance, The Chinese University of Hong Kong, 2018 (c).

———. "What Makes China Grow?" In Peter Pauly, ed., *Global Economic Modeling*. Singapore: World Scientific Publishing Company, 2018 (d), pp. 182–233.

———. "The Great Transformation—East." *Financial and Economic Review: The Lamfalussy Lectures Conference Logbook 2018* 17, no. 2. Budapest: Magyar Nemzeti Bank (Central Bank of Hungary), forthcoming (a).

———. "The Sources of Chinese Economic Growth Since 1978." In Martin Guzman, ed., *Towards a Just Society: Joseph Stiglitz and 21st Century Economics*. New York: Columbia University Press, forthcoming (b).

Lau, Lawrence J., Xikang Chen and Yanyan Xiong. "Adjusted China-U.S. Trade Balance." Working Paper No. 54, Lau Chor Tak Institute of Global Economics and Finance, The Chinese University of Hong Kong, 2017.

Lau, Lawrence J., Xikang Chen, Cuihong Yang, Leonard K. Cheng, Kwok-Chiu Fung, Yun-Wing Sung, Kunfu Zhu, Jiansuo Pei and Zhipeng Tang. *Fei jingzheng xing touru zhanyong chanchu moxing ji qi yingyong—Zhong Mei maoyi shuncha toushi* 非競爭型投入佔用產出模型及其應用——中美貿易順差透視 (Non-competitive input-output model and its application—An examination of the China-U.S. trade surplus). *Zhongguo shehui kexue (Social Sciences in China)* 28, no. 5 (October 2007), pp. 91–103.

———. "Input-Occupancy-Output Models of the Non-Competitive Type and Their Application—An Examination of the China-U.S. Trade Surplus." *Social Sciences in China* 31, no. 1 (February 2010), pp. 35–54.

Lau, Lawrence J., Yingyi Qian and Gerard Roland. "Reform without Losers: An Interpretation of China's Dual-Track Approach to Transition." *The Journal of Political Economy* 108, no. 1 (February 2000), pp. 120–143.

Lau, Lawrence J. and Junjie Tang. "The Impact of U.S. Imports from China on U.S. Consumer Prices and Expenditures." Working Paper No. 66, Lau Chor Tak Institute of Global Economics and Finance, The Chinese University of Hong Kong, 2018.

Lau, Lawrence J. and Yanyan Xiong. "Are There Laws of Innovation?: Part I, Introduction." Working Paper, Lau Chor Tak Institute of Global Economics and Finance, The Chinese University of Hong Kong, 2018.

Lau, Lawrence J., Yongjun Zhang and Shaojun Zeng. "Evolving Economic Complementarity between the U.S. and China." In China–United States Exchange Foundation, *U.S.-China in 2022: U.S.-China Economic Relations in the Next Ten Years—Towards Deeper Engagement and Mutual Benefit*. Hong Kong: China–United States Exchange Foundation, 2013, pp. 73–85.

Li, Cheng. *Chinese Politics in the Xi Jinping Era: Reassessing Collective Leadership*. Washington, D.C.: The Brookings Institution, 2016.

Maddison, Angus. *Phases of Capitalist Development*. Oxford: Oxford University Press, 1982.

———. *The World Economy: Vol. 1: A Millennial Perspective and Vol. 2: Historical Statistics*. Paris: Development Centre of the Organisation for Economic Cooperation and Development, 2006.

Neumann, Manfred J. M. "Seigniorage in the United States: How Much Does the U.S. Government Make from Money Production?" *Federal Reserve Bank of St. Louis Review*, March/April 1992, pp. 29–40. https://doi.org/10.20955/r.74.29-40.

Reif, L. Rafael. "China's Challenge is America's Opportunity." *The New York Times*, 8 August 2018.

Sevastopulo, Demetri and Tom Mitchell. "U.S. Considered Ban on Student Visas for Chinese Nationals." *Financial Times*, 2 October 2018.

United States Department of State. *United States Relations with China: With Special Reference to the Period 1944–1949*. Washington, D.C.: U.S. Government Printing Office, 1949.